PUTTING A NEW FACE ON GOD

How you see God shapes your life

Bob Hunter

All Scripture quotations, unless otherwise indicated, are taken from the Holy Bible, New International Version®, NIV®. Copyright ©1973, 1978, 1984, 2011 by Biblica, Inc.™ Used by permission of Zondervan. All rights reserved worldwide. www.zondervan.com The "NIV" and "New International Version" are trademarks registered in the United States Patent and Trademark Office by Biblica, Inc.™

© 2024 by Bob Hunter

ALL RIGHTS RESERVED
Plungefaith Publishing, Mesa, AZ.

ISBN: 9798892831581 (Print)
ISBN: 9798892832076 (eBook)

Inquiry: info@plungefaith.com

No part of this publication may be reproduced, stored in a retrieval system, or transmitted in any form by any means—electronic, mechanical, photocopying, recording or otherwise—without prior written consent of Bob Hunter, except as provided by the United States of America copyright law.

To my children and someday their children.

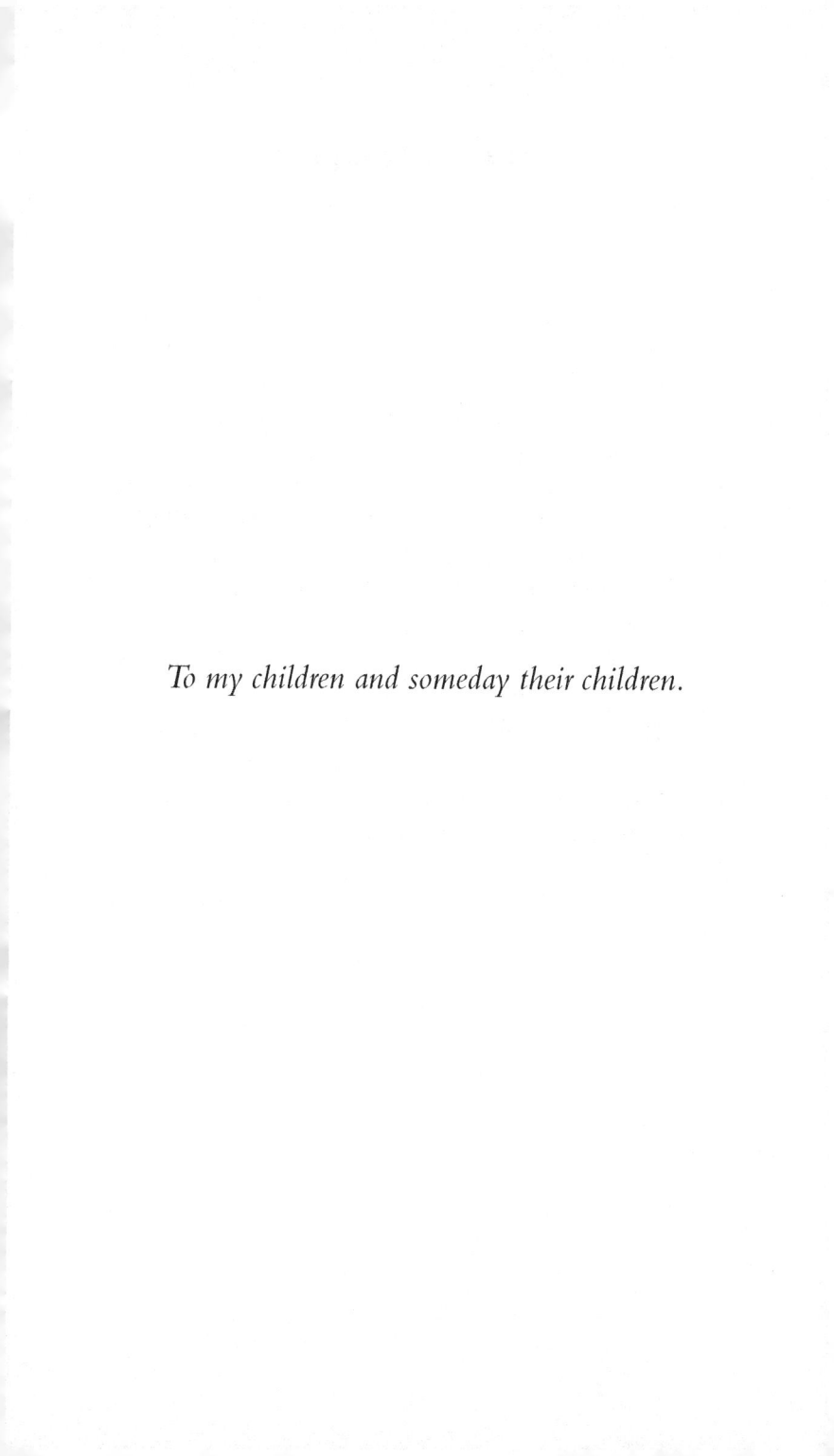

Acknowledgments

My gratefulness extends to a fantastic team of supporters, readers, and editors! I'm grateful to: Linda Dodge for being a faithful contributor, editor, and friend for many years. Charles Christian for scholarly insights and suggestions. Jeff Skinner for publishing input. Jonathan Foster for editing. My Nazarene Pastor cohort consisting of John Hanna, Angie Bentley, Angela Wilson, Christy Williams, Brandon Brown, and Jeffrey Brown. Debra Peck for inspiration. Bud Pugh for wisdom. My pastors, Brett & Tara Smith, for their support. Crossroads Church for being a "Good news community." Rip'd 4 Life guys for reverse mentoring. Dana Hicks for being an author buddy. The Kurtis & John show for smiles. And to all those who read an early copy of the manuscript and commented, I am grateful. Most of all, I thank my wife, Cambria, for supporting me as I pursue another dream.

Contents

Introduction: How you see God shapes your life 6

1. The blurring of God's face 16
2. The face of a cruel God 30
3. The face of Good News........................... 39
4. The face of God when I face my emotions 50
5. The face of a partnering God..................... 59
6. The face of God bleeds mercy................................ 70
7. The face of God who comes near 80
8. The face of a healing God........................ 90
9. The face of justice................................. 103
10. Helping others put a new face on God................. 115
11. Final blessing: The face of God shines now and forever 123
12. Today's big question: What is God like? 129

Afterword 134

Introduction
HOW YOU SEE GOD SHAPES YOUR LIFE

The title of this book may have caught your attention. Putting a new face on God? Does God need a new face? Isn't God the same yesterday, today, and forever? Does God even have a face?

Throughout the ages, many have yearned to see God. Perhaps the most renowned is a biblical figure named Moses. The book of Exodus recounts several instances of actual conversations between Moses and God. Moses is said to have visited a tent to intercede on behalf of God's people, and it was there he saw God as if he were in a face-to-face meeting with a friend (Exodus 33:11). Later in the same chapter, Moses again sought God's glory. In this instance, he was only permitted to see God's back. These profound encounters with the divine leave us with more questions than answers. Does God have a literal face and back? Was Moses able to catch a glimpse of God? Can God truly be seen? The mystery of God's existence and our attempts to comprehend who God is continue to captivate us.

Other accounts in the Bible and Christian history describe encounters with God, but few make the audacious claim to have actually seen God. But what if we are all seeing God? Not necessarily in a face-to-face manner, but in our minds? Is it possible we all perceive God in some fashion or another? And what if those images we have of God shape our lives?

This book attempts to answer those questions. For centuries, the Church has studied the nature and character of God and articulated theological statements describing who God is. These statements can be difficult for an ordinary person to understand. The doctrines of God form belief systems by which various religious denominations organize themselves. Statements describing God's character are needed to pass a faith tradition from one generation to the next. Scholars debate, dissect, and analyze these statements to determine if they fit within the orthodox framework. This book will not pursue those matters in a formal sense. Instead of debating doctrine and belief systems, people's perceptions of God will be examined. Unhelpful ones will be discarded, and new ones will be constructed in hopes our lives will become a stunning reflection of who God is.

I first came to this study in my youth. As a spiritual infant, I wrestled with the question: What is God like? Unlike some friends and classmates, I did not grow up in a church environment where God was explained to me. Without a true mentor, I tried to figure it out independently. I formulated a view of God based on fragmental bits of teaching I received and some of my own personal experiences. At times, it was a terrifying journey! What if God is angry? What if God doesn't understand me? Questions raced through my mind that needed answers. I had some gut instincts about God, but they were unrefined; I needed more.

Fast forward to my early twenties. I am a seminary student in Kansas City, MO, and I still think about what God is like, but from the perspective of formal theological studies. It was then a book written by Professor Dr. James D. Hamilton was handed to me. His book, similarly titled to this one, explored the faces of God and the inner perceptions humans have of God. Fascinated by this idea, I digested every word. Dr. Hamilton brilliantly claimed that our mental images of God essentially determine our relationships and the scope of our religion. He wasn't the first to propose this thesis and won't be the last. Despite not being a bestseller, this now out-of-print gem remained a cherished part of my library, its groundbreaking thesis continuing to resonate with me. Though now deceased, the author's exploration of this concept struck a chord deep within me. How people see God is life-shaping! While we may not see God literally, our minds feast on images, and we naturally assign mental pictures to the person of God. God is a relational being, and our relationship with God has a face. It's that simple and that profound. Faith is a visual construct.

I did a little digging to learn more about the book's history. I contacted one of Dr. Hamilton's surviving sons, and he told me his dad drew inspiration to write the book from living in Colorado for many years and retreating to the Rocky Mountain wilderness. Dr. Hamilton was known as a thoughtful and humble man who dared to ponder the question: What is God like? He recorded his insights, as I have recorded mine, in order to share them with others. Perhaps the book you are now reading will help you in the way that Dr. Hamilton's book helped me.

Formal doctrines and beliefs articulated by the Church are important, but not more important than how we actually see God and operate in the realm of faith. The images we each carry impact our emotional health, interpersonal relationships, and, ultimately, the trajectory of our spiritual journey. When did you last pause to reflect on how you see God?

The human brain is a visual machine and functions best using images. Before the age of digital media and modern graphics, much more was left to our imaginations. Our brains supplied an image to associate with characters in a book or voices on the radio. Though these faces are "real" to the reader or listener, they can differ for any two people. In the present day, images are everywhere. To illustrate this idea further, imagine your favorite novel is made into a movie. Comparisons between how you perceive a character in a book and how the movie portrays that figure consume your mind. Our brains assign images to particular character descriptions, and we sometimes experience disappointment when they do not match the characters we see on the screen.

The need to supply God with a face exists in each human brain. Although God is Spirit and therefore invisible, we make God visible by producing a mental image. The visual part of our brain paints a picture based on many things, including life experiences, cultural orientation, and religious instruction. Those mental images influence how our faith functions and how we go about our lives. Our attempts to "see" God happen consciously and subconsciously. It's both mysterious and explainable. Rational and emotional. We were created to think about God, and how we do that using images can help us become the best version of ourselves.

The images we carry of God are tailored to our uniqueness. Those images can range from an angry Judge to seeing God as a Santa Claus figure without a naughty list. But God always has a face; indeed, many faces, as an old Hindu proverb proclaimed. The basic idea of the book you are reading is this: humanly speaking, God has a million faces! This may explain why so many people across the globe express a unique sense of faith in God, leading to Christianity's emergence as the first truly global religion. Could it be the Christian invitation to be transformed by a vision of God took hold? Soon we will venture into the biblical text and examine how our individual perceptions can reflect the rich history of God's faithfulness. But for now, the human experience of putting a face to God is important to explore.

Throughout my life journey, I have encountered several people who wrestle with negative images of God. For many, God is angry and unpredictable. "I see God as authoritarian," said one person. "God is very demanding, always pushing me to do more than my capabilities," said another. "I never know if what I'm doing results in God punishing me or rewarding me," yet another individual said. How did these views come about? Where do we get these impressions?

Distorted perceptions of God often stem from the inner turmoil and conflicts we experience in life. During moments of acute pain, it's natural to turn to God, questioning our faith in the process. The familiar cry of "Why me, God?" echoes in times of desperation, challenging our beliefs. Human suffering becomes the ultimate test of faith, forcing us to reconcile our understanding of God with the harsh realities of life. If God is angry and unpredictable, you might be inclined to think you are being punished for poor performance. If God is the instigator of pain and the author of human suffering for ultimate good, you might conclude you are not good enough and God has rough edges to polish. Sometimes, our view of God compounds our pain and delays our healing. Indeed, human suffering reveals beliefs that we have harbored all along. No wonder so many people are walking away from faith these days. A God who allows all these terrible things to transpire for our good is a God unworthy of our complete trust. In fact, such versions of God make atheism an attractive alternative.

What is God like? The question is the same for everyone. One might think only unbelievers assign negativity to God, but that is not the case. I've engaged dozens of Christian believers who openly struggle to put a better face on God. Instead of love, fear is a determining factor in their operation of faith. While this may sound outrageous, I have encountered people outside the faith with a better view of God than others from within. It's hard to fathom how this could be possible, but it makes sense when you consider the baggage organized religion brings and the impoverished images of God preached right from our pulpits. Whether you have no faith, are new to faith, or have been around for a while, I hope you will wrestle with some of the ideas in this book and progress toward a healthier, more sustainable view of God. Answering critical questions about God's character is a fundamental part of life.

Let's do a preliminary exercise before going any further. Write a personal reflection essay outlining your inner perceptions of God. Avoid traditional Sunday School answers and quotes from famous Christians; state your view of God in the simplest terms. Ask yourself: *How am I seeing God? Who is God to me?* Because this is an exercise in your "felt concept" of God and not how much you objectively know about God, the outcome of this assignment may surprise you and disturb you.

The reason for this reflection essay? Your personal perception of God is the "real" God of your life. The version of God you operate with has a conceptual framework. God, for any given person, is the God they see and experience. If your God is angry and unpredictable, your relationship with God and others will function according to those values. If your God is loving and benevolent, the likelihood of consistently exhibiting those values is exceptionally high. The way you see God shapes your life and defines your relationships. As your view of God rises, so does your spiritual health and well-being.

Real-life examples illustrate the powerful truth of how we see God. Let's start with a young man named Manuel. Pornography consumption is his battle. "I feel that God thinks I'm naughty," he says. Manuel grew up in a church that taught the goodness of God and the beauty of salvation in Christ. However, on a subjective level, he feels unworthy of that beauty and goodness because of the addiction gripping his soul. His self-image suffers along with his feelings about God. His emotions keep score, resulting in considerable shame, guilt, and depression.

Where does Manuel go from here, and how can we help? Manuel must be reminded that God will not crush him for falling into a sinful habit. Feeling unworthy of God's love is a natural byproduct of porn consumption, or any addiction for that matter. Porn's lies deeply mar the face of God's love on a subjective level. God, however, is bigger than a porn habit, and redeeming love can break through filth and false perceptions. Recovery from the impoverishment that porn brings into one's life is needed on a large scale in society, and it begins with an understanding of love's transformative power and the sin-penetrating qualities of God's grace. Manuel is a good candidate for this renewed vision, and so are many others. Replacing a God who condemns with a God who loves and rescues is needed. Of course, we want Manuel to get professional help, but we also want him to lean into a view of God that will guide his recovery instead of compounding the shame.

As with many persons with a negative view of God, how they view themselves is deeply affected. Take Allison, for example. She routinely feels terrible about herself and projects those feelings onto God. She confesses, "I don't think God likes me because I'm not good enough." Allison's problems are rooted in the statement, "I'm not good enough," leading to desperate attempts to please God or give up altogether. Assuming Allison continues on this trajectory, at what point will she be good enough? The obvious answer is never. It is like the fable of the donkey and the carrot. The dangling carrot in front of the donkey is always out of reach. The reward is visible and desirable, and for the donkey, all it takes is a few more steps, but the reward is still the same distance away after all that effort. What drives this behavior? Feelings of unworthiness and low self-esteem. It's a common trap. The notion that a person's unworthiness is cured by working harder and taking a few more steps is totally false.

Allison elaborates on her struggles with God, "I feel God is keeping score, and I'm not making the cut; if life is a test, I'm failing. Something must be wrong with me, and I don't feel close to God." Allison relates to God based on performance. Her God is always beyond her reach and never satisfied. The internal struggle and conflict embedded in her view of God cause tremendous pain. How can Allison be in a relationship with a God who doesn't think she's good enough? The face she puts on God is unpleasable.

She's not alone in adopting this dangerous mindset. Sometimes, it is hard to discern whether a person's low self-esteem skews their perception of God or if a negative view of God produces a low sense of self-esteem. We may not resolve that tension entirely, but working toward a solution is possible.

Several semi-fictional examples are used in this book to help readers identify the problems we encounter seeing God. Perhaps you can relate to Allison, who seeks God's approval and love through better performance. Or, like Manuel, you find yourself trapped in an addictive lifestyle that makes you feel unworthy of God's love. You may feel stranded in a gap between what you know and what you experience in real life. You objectively believe God is loving and good, but your personal experience doesn't match what you believe. There are traps and gaps everywhere in life. Being aware of them and working to avoid them is a wise undertaking. The good news of recovery is woven into the pages of this book. Negative images can be replaced with positive ones, producing the best version of you while improving your relationship with God.

Imagine a redemptive outcome for both Manuel and Allison. Manuel submits to an addiction recovery program and finds freedom from porn's grip on his soul. His recovery is enhanced by a renewed vision of God, who comes to people in their darkest moments and lifts them out of the poverty of sin. Instead of being met with condemnation, Manuel finds a friend in God to guide his recovery. Allison journeys down a different path. After many years of striving for God's approval, she reaches a breaking point and quits. She quits attending a local church, reading her Bible, and calling herself a Christian because she feels unworthy of the label. But that's not the end of

Allison's story; she finds hope and healing in a God who visits people who have given up. For many years, Allison worshipped a God of achievement instead of one who values a person's worth. When her false version of God collapsed, leaving her faith shattered, she came to a new understanding. No longer a slave to an unpleasable God, Allison's life is now transformed with joy and servanthood. Instrumental in both stories: A new face on God.

For readers who claim no faith at all, I hope you continue with this book. Wisdom from a Catholic priest sum up my intentions, "I do not think it is preposterous to believe in God, I am just hoping people stop believing in a preposterous God." The face we put on God, in some instances, is a God who doesn't exist, and there are many of them in circulation. Because we see God a certain way, it is entirely possible that the images we have of God hold us back. The God of some believing Christians is not one I believe in. Such versions of God are not even Christian; they are preposterous and fraudulent. One biblical author described false gods as being powerless and stationary. Shiny and attractive at first, those gods eventually prove themselves helpless, heavy, and tone-deaf (Isaiah 46). Isn't it time we relieve ourselves of these burdens? If we follow Him, Jesus invites us to cast down those burdens, *"My yoke is easy, my burden is light"* (Matthew 11:30). A burdensome God is no kind of God to carry. Life is too short. Before you write off faith in God as a viable path in life, consider whether or not the God of your understanding is real or a rogue human perception. There's always a chance any one of us could be wrong.

Chapter One
The blurring of God's face

Blurred, marred, and distorted are fitting words to describe many people's view of God. For the most part, we enter into this world with a blank spiritual slate. But along the way, our perspective on God evolves for better or worse. For worse, because of the human capacity to mismanage, misperceive, and mishandle information about God. Indeed, God would not burden humans with such negativity from birth that years of recovery would be required. When it comes to God, the blurring we see is a product of something else. God does a fantastic job of self-disclosure in the Bible. God's version of God-self is clear enough to invite men and women into a vibrant relationship, but God is not responsible for the flawed ways in which people think about God. As a famous thinker once said, "To err is human."

The title of this chapter, *The Blurring of God's Face*, is an unfortunate reality. I have chosen the word 'blur' because it speaks to a familiar problem. Imagine driving your car down a dusty dirt road in the country. After a few minutes of travel, a thin layer of dirt accumulates on the surface of your car's windshield. You are about to hit the onramp to do highway driving, but you can't see very well. What now? A stop at the first available filling station can help. Most gas pumps have windshield washing equipment nearby to clean vehicle glass. After a few quick swipes, your visibility is restored, making it safe to proceed as planned. Something similar happens in the blurring of God's face. Unflattering inaccurate views of God, regardless of their source, accumulate, clouding our vision. These views subconsciously influence how we think, feel, and act. The unnecessary film is removable if we are willing to endure the rigors of spiritual growth and remove the layers of dust needed to see God more clearly.

Blurry-faced versions of God that are angry, unpredictable, and unsympathetic collect on our spiritual windshield. These blurred versions of God afflict instead of affirm. Life events feel more like punishment instead of privileged opportunities for growth. An obstructed spiritual windshield produces versions of God that hamper our development as humans. How did this vision impairment come about? At what point did God's face become blurred?

The flattened tire example is where we will start to uncover some answers. Take yourself back to the dusty, dirty road. This time with low tire pressure. After a couple hours of travel, you have a blowout and find yourself stranded alongside the road, needing help. In the heat of the moment, you jump to all kinds of hasty conclusions. You rationalize that the adversity you are facing is God getting back at you for not being a good person. You conflate your understanding of Karma with God and the belief that what goes around comes around. You bargain with God to do better and pledge to pray more consistently. The subconscious part of your brain starts deal-making, "God, if you get me out of this one, I'll pay you back generously."

Is the above example overdone? I don't think so. This is the view many persons have of God—a transactional deal-making God. There are downsides to this way of thinking. Filtering life events through the lens of a God who punishes some and rewards others based on deal-making ability is pretty harsh. A God who wheels and deals on the fly could never be entirely just. How can a person genuinely worship a bribe-taking God? The working logic goes like this, "God, I'll give you fill-in-the-blank if you get me out of this mess." For some perspective on the matter, all tires eventually go flat, which is a normal part of vehicle ownership. Roadside breakdowns are neither caused nor prevented by God. They are often the result of failed equipment, human oversight, and driver misjudgment. Is God's assistance available in these crisis moments? Absolutely! But God is not the causal agent or the immediate solution. Think of it like this: God doesn't fix flat tires but works through people who do. Clarifying who is responsible for what in the ordeal is helpful. In a later chapter, we'll discuss the boundary lines between what God does and what we do.

Versions of God, such as this one, are not a sudden occurrence. Blurred mindsets develop over time and typically stem from poor information sources or none at all. Religious authority figures, family members, and media sources feed us images, right or wrong, that shape our thoughts and influence our lives. We're going to touch on a few of those in this chapter.

The blurring process begins in early childhood and is unusually potent during those years. From there, blurred images persist through adulthood despite a person's good intentions. You may not even be aware that it is happening. Once those assumptions are acquired, precious time and effort are needed to cancel their influence. They didn't come to you overnight, nor will they be corrected in a short manner of speaking.

Here's something else to consider: Our prayers and discussions about God reflect our true beliefs. Every word we utter, every phrase we articulate, is a window opened to our thinking. The term "theology" itself, stemming from the Greek "theos" (God) and "logos" (word), underscores the profound connection between our language and our understanding of God. Our God-speak improves as better understandings are sought with more defined terminology. Much like tending to a plant in a garden, nurturing our theology in the rich soil of our soul yields an abundant harvest. Conversely, neglect and malnutrition can cause it to wither. Cultivating a theology rooted in love that grows continuously should always be our goal.

To illustrate our theology's growth potential, let's look at another struggle many have with God. Derived directly from Scripture, the phrase "God the Father" is hard for people to grasp. The face of God as "father" for those abandoned and traumatized by their earthly fathers is brutal. "If God is like my earthly father, then I don't see how I can believe," said one person. Does that mean we eliminate references to God the Father? Not necessarily. Properly defining the terms while striving to overcome the emotional triggers associated with the idea is a fitting place to start. Problems with God's father-ness are not new; throughout history, many great persons of faith have battled.

Martin Luther, the great Church reformer of the 16th century, was one of those individuals. His theology of God's fatherhood came under siege when he was a young boy because of the harsh ways in which his biological father parented. He grew up in a home where minor offenses aroused swift disciplinary responses from both parents, mostly from his father. The emotional trauma resulted in a profound disconnect between his father and him, which he then transferred to his relationship with God. The strictness and sternness his earthy father exhibited spilled over into his spiritual life. Later, Luther pressed into his faith, discovering that God was very much unlike his earthly father. Like many in contemporary times, Luther struggled with the initial phrase of the Lord's Prayer, "*Our Father in Heaven,*" amidst the shadows of his past experiences.

While many have yet to experience it, the potential exists for growth. Luther's example parallels a new generation struggling to embrace a God who Jesus identified as Abba Father. God's true character, revealed in the fertile soil of Luther's soul, helped heal some of those youthful traumas. Putting a new face on God saved Luther from missing out on one of God's special qualities. What was possible for Luther is also possible for us. Distinguishing God from our earthly father's worst qualities is a growth and healing journey than can benefit many. It takes considerable time and discipline to break away from blurred understandings of God and find clarity. Still, the reward is worth it, especially regarding something like the fatherhood of God, which I wouldn't want anyone to miss.

Other terms and descriptions of God blur our thinking. Terms like almighty, all-knowing, all-seeing, and ever-present tend to scare people because of what is implied. Who is this God that knows everything and doesn't act? If God sees and knows everything, does that mean a detailed record of my sins exists? I've done too many things wrong to be in a relationship with a God who is always right, which is how some might feel. We rarely say it out loud, but we subconsciously feel the tension. How can God claim to be almighty and not intervene to stop evil? Is God teasing us with these descriptions? Or do we say words and not understand their meaning in the truest sense?

Words and definitions have tremendous power, and regardless of their origin, their influence over how we think about God needs to be monitored. Some words used to describe God have important historical and theological meanings and contribute to a widely accepted belief system we call orthodoxy. But those terms are not exclusively static in their meaning; a certain amount of theological nuance occurs because we are dealing with human beings and their felt concept of God. Part of growing our theology calls for exploration, personal enlightenment, and discovery of new ideas. Sometimes, we are rediscovering old meanings that have unfortunately been lost through the ages. Nuance is part of every person's experience with God. Sadly, religious traditions are often inflexible and intolerant of nuance. In many instances, they hinder spiritual growth by narrowly interpreting Bible passages and insisting everyone else accept their conclusions. It pains me to say it, but the Church is one of the primary venues for blurring God's image. To illustrate, let me give a heartbreaking example.

Joseph grew up in a strict fundamentalist church where a steady stream of teachings from the book of Revelation were delivered. He vividly remembers timelines, charts, and graphs, ominously predicting the Lord's return to earth. Fiery apocalyptic images and doomsday scenarios left a permanent impression on Joseph. The church library contained a trove of books authored by so-called "prophecy" experts who claimed to teach directly from the Bible. The face Joseph puts on God is one of razor-thin patience and righteous indignation. Unapologetically, his religious tradition promoted a hard-nosed version of God, and the label of "heretic" was applied to anyone in opposition. Joseph refers to himself as a recovering wrath-aholic. Why? Because he was taught to live in a panicked state of readiness for the Lord's sudden return. Instead of loving God, his posture was one of fear and anxiety. Men and women found faithful on the day of the Lord's return obtain a generous reward; others are doomed to eternal hell, and you certainly didn't want to be among that group. Heaven's gate or hell's flames were the choices.

Joseph is a victim of God-blurring, and his faith tradition bears responsibility. Youth in Joseph's church were expected to obey rules unquestionably. Nuancing particular beliefs was not encouraged. Young people are impressionable and the messages they receive from religious teachers in those settings are generally not opposed. Joseph must heal while constructing a faith experience built on love, not fear. Hours of counseling and theological rehabilitation are needed. Joseph is now growing his faith in a positive direction. He is discovering a new perspective, a God who transforms instead of interrogates. He is a healthier person emotionally and spiritually today because of this journey. As his view of God improved, so did his life.

Religious teachers and church establishments are not always wrong; some are incredibly influential in all the right ways. Structured delivery of God-talk (theology) is instrumental in faith formation. The posture of a learner is one of implicit acceptance; after all, religious authority figures hear from God, right? Beyond reproach is how the Bible describes the duties of a teacher, meaning they must deliver correct teachings, and their lives should be consistent with those values. The implied trust a religious teacher enjoys should be handled with extreme care at all times. Sadly, that trust has been broken in far too many religious traditions, and unsuspecting learners become the subject of reckless teachings about God, yielding spiritual immaturity. If you identify with Joseph and you grew up the victim of theological malpractice and spiritual abuse, I am genuinely sorry, and I hope this book aids your recovery. But take heart: not everyone gets it wrong. Scores of faithful teachers and preachers articulate beautiful homilies describing God; their reward is the many lives they impact along the way.

Reflecting on my own journey, I am blessed to have been mentored by several men and women who deposited a rich understanding of God into my life. At the age of seventeen, as a new believer, compelling images of God were presented based on scriptural teachings that helped me form a healthy relationship with God. Thankfully, the positive messages outweighed the negative ones. And believe me, there were plenty of negative spiritual influences that I somehow managed to avoid, particularly ones using fear as a recruiting or conversion tactic.

Portrayals of God that skew negative stick in a young person's mind, eventually reaching a crisis point resulting in one of the following actions. That person will: 1) Leave the Christian faith out of frustration; 2) Live with a blurred version of God that doesn't work; 3) Do the hard work of putting a new face on God. We hope the third option is chosen. If you are presently filling the role of a teacher in a faith community, consider how your teachings about God are impressing young people. Ask yourself, *how can I reflect God more accurately?*

Let's extend this discussion using a classroom scenario. When a teacher disciplines a misbehaving class with, "God doesn't like classroom behavior that is bad," the view of a punishing God is presented. This statement can imprint deeply on impressionable children, fostering a subconscious association between God and the idea of disapproval and, possibly, retribution. This underscores the crucial role of early childhood teachers in shaping a child's faith journey within a believing community. They possess the unique ability to instill positive perceptions of God, guiding children toward a lifelong journey governed by love and not rule-keeping. Teachers need to refrain from inadvertently instilling negative connotations about God in their students' minds. While addressing misbehavior is important, using God as a tool to invoke fear may not be the most effective approach. Teachers have a responsibility to help students form a healthy image of God. This doesn't mean turning a blind eye to misconduct but rather implementing accountability, discipline, and personal boundaries in a constructive manner.

From the classroom to the pulpit, blurring concerns persist. Preached sermons, in particular, convey profoundly influential information about God, but preachers don't always get it right, and blurred images of God seep into listeners' minds. Once, I heard a preacher use an Old Testament story illustrating a priest entering the Holy of Holies with a rope fastened around his foot in the event God were to strike him dead. This preacher connected that idea to a passage in the New Testament book of Acts where two people were caught defrauding the early church of a promised gift, which prompted a tragic sequence of events costing them their lives (Acts 5). I would describe the sermon as an overzealous attempt to communicate

God's power, holiness, and righteousness. Unfortunately, it created more heat than light, startling listeners with descriptions of God that are angry and unpredictable. Well-meaning preachers and not-so-well-meaning preachers deliver faulty messages concerning God's true character, and those images become cemented in our minds, producing shallow faith and, in some cases, atheism.

The next stop on our journey is the homes in which we grew up. Teachers have great significance, but much of our thinking about God is influenced by what happens in the home. Our parents represent God in the example they set and the words they speak, which can feel like an overwhelming responsibility because it probably is. A parent's understanding of God is usually passed to children, and blurry images of God get handed down to the next generation.

The sacred duty of parenting is God ordained and we owe it to our children to convey a healthy image of God that will yield a life marked by love. Far too often, children totally reject their youth's faith tradition (option #1 on the list provided above). In some cases, they have legitimate reasons for doing so. Children growing up in homes where religious hypocrisy and fear-based parenting methods were present become victims. Rather than blame young people for their lack of faith, thoughtful reflection and personal resolve are needed to grow our theology more positively. Ask yourself, if you are a parent, *how can I become the best reflection of God to my children?* It's never too late to reduce the blurs and portray a better image of God. The most impactful gift we can offer our children is our own healing from distorted images of God.

Society in general is another source of influence shaping one's view of God. Social media, in particular, plays a significant role in young people's lives, and let's face it, a lot of intentional blurring goes on there. God is often parodied on social media platforms in a manner that generates mockery, which is not anything new. The scene familiar to most is of a terror-stricken offender appearing before the judgment throne of God in an atmosphere of clouds awaiting an eternal sentence. Older forms of media like newspapers, comic strips, and television sitcoms invoked those images, too. St. Peter is standing at the pearly gates, God is on the throne, and judgment is rendered. The face of God, according to these sources? Scowling with anger while a verdict is reached. People of religious faith are portrayed worse. Intolerant fools living in some alternate reality form is often the context. It's very disheartening; downright malicious attacks are leveled against people of faith and their God. These images leave a lasting impression and not for the better.

Modern news outlets also play a role in how our theology is shaped. When natural disasters strike, the media will often report the accounts of victims or near victims of a tragic event from which all kinds of theological reasoning flows. Anything from "It must have been the will of God." To "Thank God I was spared because I prayed…" The latter is a big problem because it creates assumptions about non-praying people perishing due to their lack of faith. How cruel is that? What kind of God would favor some and not others? News outlets are not the only ones; the insurance industry uses a clause stating coverage for damage deemed an "act of God" is a valid claim. In a legal manner of speaking, provisions are offered to compensate for God's bad behavior. As you can see, blurry-faced portrayals of God abound in almost every domain of life.

Many other information sources shape or blur our view of God. We would be hard-pressed to name them all, but by naming a few, we can better understand how our thinking about God is cemented at an early age and continues throughout adulthood. We enter the world as blank slates, yet as we navigate life's journey, we accumulate perceptions of God that become ingrained within us. Consequently, what we internalize about God inevitably manifests in our outward behaviors and attitudes. All those faces we put on God, especially the frightening and demanding ones, seep out of our lives and determine our level of faith and maturity. People tend to reflect the God they worship.

The point of this chapter is that if God's face has become blurred, it can also become unblurred. If our spiritual windshield has become cloudy, maybe it's time to remove the film. Will we have a perfect vision of God? No, but it can improve, and as it does, so will our lives. The Apostle Paul said it this way: *"For now we see only a reflection as in a mirror; then we shall see face to face. Now I know in part; then I shall know fully, even as I am fully known"* (1 Corinthians 13:12). What we know about God and the mental images we form are small glimpses in comparison to what will be revealed to us at a future time. We see little snippets for now, but a lot more is coming! Reflections of God are still visible in every corner of human existence that will one day culminate in a grand unveiling. In the meantime, God can be seen and known with increasing clarity if we set our hearts to it. Our job is to be the best managers possible of what God has disclosed to us.

Unblurring, unmasking, and unblaming God are vital spiritual formation strategies. I do not think naively about it; putting a new face on God may be years in the making, so don't be discouraged if you do not see progress immediately. It's terrifying at first, but freedom awaits. The spiritual exercises at the end of each chapter exist to guide your journey. I hope you will reflect on the ideas presented and wrestle with seeing God more clearly.

Spiritual Formation

- Our deeply impressionable souls are stamped with images of God that stay with us, affecting our lives for good or ill. In light of this reality and our chapter on blurring, take some time to reflect on your journey. In a journal entry, ask yourself, *Who or what influenced my thinking about God the most? Did that influence produce a positive or negative view of God? How has that influence stayed with me? Where do I go from here?*

- Your father figure growing up likely influenced how you relate to God the Father. Who was your father figure growing up? You may have none, or one, or several males who impacted your life, and they may include a birth, adoptive, or foster father; a teacher, a pastor or youth pastor; an uncle or grandparent; a neighbor, a family friend, a coach, or a father of a friend. Note: circle any of the father figures from the list above, or write the name of someone else here:

- You may want to divide your journaling page into three columns. In the left column, write down the name of the person or group that influenced your thinking about God; in the middle column, write words, concepts, or beliefs that you internalized from that person or relationship; in the right column, note whether their influence in a specific area was positive or negative, and how it impacts you today.

- If you are a teacher or a parent, consider your role as someone who reflects God's image. How does your instruction and example set the stage for young people to see the face of God? What are you doing to ensure you depict God in a manner that is consistent with a God of love and transformation?

- Portrayals of God that skew negative create three options for people: 1) Leaving the Christian faith out of frustration; 2) Living with a blurred version of God that doesn't work; 3) Doing the hard work of putting a new face on God. Where do you find yourself? Which option best describes your faith journey?

Chapter Two
The face of a cruel God

How did God get to be like that? There's no way around it; the Bible contains disturbing descriptions of God. In some instances, God is portrayed as a stone-cold killer. Particularly in the Old Testament before the coming of Christ, God seems responsible for genocide, cruelty to women and children, and ritual sacrifices. It's hard to relate to this kind of God; many rightly object to it. The face of God in the Old Testament is cruel to the modern reader. Rather than hide from it, let's deal with it.

The first big act of God's cruelty comes in Genesis Chapter 6, where God destroys the earth and all its inhabitants during the great flood. Only Noah and his family survive; everyone else perishes. Many other cruel episodes follow. Though not as catastrophic but still cruel, God commanded Joshua to conquer the city of Jericho, leading an army of 40,000 to encircle it and drive out all its inhabitants. Only Rahab and her family survive the devastation. The armies of the Philistines didn't fare much better; God's people slaughtered them because God commanded the faithful to wipe out entire populations in cold blood. Cruel acts are attributed to God in the Old

Testament. Either God really is this way, or there must be another way to think about these events in the context of the biblical story.

It's entirely possible for the average Bible reader to take these cruel episodes at face value and conclude God is harsh and unforgiving: God gets revenge, God instigates wars, God wipes out whole nations, etc. If cruel episodes are read in the "plain sense" of reading, then it is easy to connect the dots and assume God is still cruel today. In case you aren't familiar with it, the plain sense of reading goes like this: If I read it in the Bible and it makes sense to me, it must, therefore, be true. After all, the Bible is the Bible, and it has to be believed in its entirety. The plain sense of reading might be an appropriate way to read some books, but it doesn't do justice to a book with so many layers of complexity. Hopefully, this chapter can help readers overcome those difficulties because worshipping a cruel God is repugnant.

Why does it seem God acts so harshly in the Old Testament? Tackling that question is not an easy task. I offer three explanations; I'm sure there are more, but let's start with some basics. First, some God-blurring likely transpired because the biblical authors were human, and their words reflect a way of life that is foreign to us. Early figures in the Bible's history were not privy to modern literary tools and advanced understandings, and they tried to build a record of God's revelation according to their best abilities under extremely harsh living conditions. These accounts, spread over centuries, depict God speaking to ordinary people amid their deepest struggles. Life in ancient Mesopotamia was marked by a quest for survival, tribal warfare, and constant bloodshed. It's hard to imagine a scenario where this way of life didn't rub off on how the authors viewed God. Think of it: biblical authors were charged with the difficult task of recording the sacred scriptures without any qualifications other than willingness, and they often did this while fighting for their lives. Given these circumstances, it's remarkable that we have clarity in the revelatory accounts and call these stories "inspired."

Secondly, emotions got in the way. The Bible contains a lot of unfiltered emotion in both testaments. Writers in the Old Testament put it all out there. Fits of anger, cries for justice, and depressed rants are recorded in the Bible's pages. As such, it is very possible for the biblical authors to have portrayed God in ways heavily influenced by the intensity of their emotions. King David is a prime example. Author of many of the Psalms, he rips into God, breaks down crying, and expresses fear he will die if God doesn't kill his enemies. It was real, raw, and authentic. David's emotions were palpable, which may have colored his interpretation of God. Does that sound familiar? When we are overwhelmed with emotion, everything gets blown out of proportion in the heat of the moment. While some of David's psalms are a flood of emotion, others seem rational and convey stunning proclamations of God's goodness and mercy. I'm not making excuses for biblical authors; I am saying the emotional magnitude of what was going on must be acknowledged. Other biblical books, like Jeremiah, were recorded while shedding profuse tears. Jeremiah was known as the weeping prophet because his oracles were lament-filled. Prophets especially didn't hold back, and intense emotions likely influenced their view of God, which they then recorded.

Thirdly, cultural factors and influences from other ancient gods were in the mix. Alongside the God depicted in the Bible, numerous rival gods existed. The blending of belief systems, called syncretism, was a problem, and sometimes faithful God-followers were guilty of integrating the characteristics of those gods with their own accounts. How do I know this happened? The Bible contains internal evidence it occurred. The faithful were influenced in a wrong way by other gods, and the worship of other gods rubbed off on their understanding. Many Old Testament narratives saw the ongoing struggle to preserve a true revelatory account of God without any encumbrances. I'm not entirely sure the right version of God won out in some instances.

The factors outlined above give a brief overview of how Old Testament accounts of God came into existence—especially painfully dark ones. At the time of writing, biblical authors were unaware their words would carry so much weight in interpreting God some 2,500 to 3,000 years later. They gave personal, unfiltered accounts of God with many human factors in play, and God was okay with that. God refused to seize the pen and set the record straight. Despite human factors, divine inspiration visited these authors, and their accounts of God were still included in the official collection of books we call the canon. The Bible is an honest book revealing all of our humanity and all of God's divinity. On the human side, it is evident to readers that even the faithful struggle to see God. Many Old Testament prophets and priests strived for wisdom in discerning God more correctly, a striving that persists today. Make no mistake; we are progressing toward a fuller revelation of God despite our many struggles.

An old English pastor formulated a prayer that captures the spirit of this journey; it is known as the famous Triple Prayer, which I will refer to often: *"O most merciful Redeemer,*

Friend, and Brother, of you three things I pray: To see you more clearly, love you more dearly, follow you more nearly, day by day" (Richard of Chichester 1197-1253). The biblical authors, often portraying God as cruel, were no exception. They were struggling within themselves to distill God's true nature, and along the way, misperceptions, raw emotion, and other influences played a role. Despite where they may have failed, they sought God wholeheartedly and yearned to know God better. Little did they know, their accounts set the stage for a new revelation to eclipse all others, making it possible for millions across the spectrum of time to put a better face on God. The Old Testament paved the way for the New.

Another critical factor to consider is this: the nature of the Holy Scriptures and the nature of God are separate. When we can't distinguish between these two things, we have trouble understanding God, and a number of fiascoes, debates, and arguments ensue. Far too many people read the Bible at face value and fail to make the distinction between what is being written about God and God's own being. The Bible is an inspired book, but it does not outrank the person of Christ when it comes to describing God. A wise seminary professor once told his class, *"The Bible is the manger in which Christ is laid."* I am not diminishing the Bible's role in our formation; I am trying to explain its nature and purpose. The Bible is not our salvation, nor is it an object of worship; it is a valuable tool in guiding us on our journey. Yes, it contained an inspired account, but with many layers of complexity that require understanding the socio-cultural factors in play to fully grasp the authors' intent. If all that seems too complicated, don't worry; by focusing on Jesus, you'll never miss a beat.

The new tradition is Jesus, who is the "Word" made flesh! A clearer picture of God comes to us in the person of Christ. Jesus gave us the proper lens through which to see God. All remaining concerns about God's cruelty are sufficiently answered in Christ, a man of sorrows who exhibited pure goodness and holy love. The arrival of Christ ushers in a new era of revelation, which the faithful call the New Testament or the New Covenant. The Old Testament spends much of its time anticipating this development and hoping for a Messiah. Jesus' coming to earth fulfills that hope, giving us a more complete picture of God.

Some of my words here may anger some religious people because they desperately want the Old Testament and New Testament to stand on equal ground. Insisting the Old Testament has the same authority as the New Testament goes something like this: "The Bible is the Bible, it's all important, every ounce of it should be preached." That sounds logical until you level it up with the person of Christ. In Jesus' most famous sermon, the Sermon on the Mount, he dismantled portions of the Old Testament with newly revealed truth. He repeatedly said, *"You've heard it said...but I say unto you..."* Christ didn't abolish previous accounts of God; instead, he fulfilled them in his life, death, and resurrection, allowing us to get to know God better. Revelation is a dynamic, forward-moving trajectory. In other words, the Bible is not flat, it rises through a series of installments. Early recipients received an initial installment, Moses and the prophets were privy to a fuller measure, and finally, Christ came to earth as the perfect God-revealer. We put more weight on what has been revealed in the New Testament. A more vivid account, a better picture, and a clearer revelation are found there. The notion that all Scripture is equal doesn't hold up for that reason.

The book of Hebrews in the New Testament describes the seismic shift from the Old Testament to the New Testament and how it enhances our view of God. Chapters 1-4 claim Jesus is the ultimate revelation, better than Moses, the angels, and the high priests. In this way, a new era of mercy is born. According to Hebrews 2:17, *"He became human in every way that he might become merciful."* In other words, Jesus is the full embodiment of mercy. With the coming of Christ, everything changes. I do not see the arrival of Jesus as the end of God's cruelty; I see it as God's way of telling us He may not have been all that cruel in the first place! God's revelation gets sweeter with time, and the goodness of God displayed in Christ is the new standard. With the visibility of Christ, a more beautiful painting of God's true character is unveiled. Whether or not we can resolve the dilemma surrounding God's cruelty, Jesus is our guide for now and forever because everything you read in the Old Testament is subject to the authority of Christ.

Thomas attends a church that affirms the equality of all scriptures in the Bible and preaches the Old Testament with just as much authority as the New Testament. His church members believe God is the same yesterday, today, and forever. Accordingly, God's promises to Abraham are available to modern believers, and when those promises are executed by faith, prosperity follows. They also believe God fights their battles and scatters their enemies because the Lord's anointed cannot be touched. Like Abraham, they faithfully bring a tenth of their income to the church to secure a blessing on the remaining ninety percent. Failure to pay the tithe removes God's favor, leaving one vulnerable to the enemy who steals and destroys. He also believes God's wrath can be applied to society's vile criminals in the form of capital punishment. His faith operates as though the message of the New Testament failed in its purpose. His God is cruel, transactional, and discriminatory. Thomas isn't alone; many have fallen prey, settling for a "B" grade Old Testament religion cloaked in the garments of Christian grace.

I wrote this book for those like Thomas and others struggling to see God. My heart goes out to the victims—men and women who have been led to believe in a God who doesn't love them for who they are and constantly monitors their every move, searching for behaviors that need modification. Promoting the idea of a cruel God based on plain sense readings of the Old Testament is profoundly misguided. God is far from cruel, as Jesus demonstrates. It's possible that the writers of the Old Testament may have attributed specific harsh actions to God for which God had no part. While there may be differing opinions on interpreting the Old Testament, what's most important is what you'll learn in the next chapter. God continues to communicate, and perceptions of cruelty will be challenged. Keep reading with an open heart.

Spiritual Formation

- If you are familiar with the Old Testament portion of the Bible, what are your favorite stories and why? What do your selections reveal about the face you put on God? How have they formed your faith positively? What passages in the Bible have invoked fear and anxiety about God? How did you resolve those fears? Who helped you wrestle with those issues?

- All readings from the Old Testament must now be put to the "Jesus test." How do Jesus' ministry and teachings help us deal with burdensome commands and laws like capital punishment, genocide, and ritual sacrifice? In what ways has the person of Christ annulled, fulfilled, or superseded some of those Old Testament traditions? How is our view of God different with Jesus as our guide now and forever?

- The Ten Commandments and other Old Testament passages may give some readers the impression God is a stickler when it comes to moral living. What is your impression? Is God patrolling the earth in search of rule-breakers? How does this view of God conflict with the person of Christ?

- Do you think it is possible that certain acts of cruelty seemingly attributed to God in the Old Testament don't accurately represent God? Is it conceivable that some Bible writers simply recorded God as cruel due to their own interpretive lenses of reality?

- Study Colossians 1: 15-18, where Jesus is portrayed as the visible face of an invisible God. In the Old Testament, men strived to see God's face but could not. Take some time to reflect on the person of Christ who represents the image of the invisible God; what new insights have you gained from reading this scripture? How will your life be different?

Chapter Three
The face of Good News

The Spirit of the Lord is on me, because he has anointed me to proclaim good news to the poor
-Luke 4:18

How about some good news? Good news reflects God's character in the purest sense. In the New Testament, the tragic story of our estrangement from God collides with a solution in Jesus Christ, fulfilling all the hopes and dreams of the Old Testament.

The delivery of a savior, appearing in human flesh, announces a new era of time and a new way of relating to God. Everything God does increases in value with time, as when Jesus arrived. Can you imagine the status of our world without a Savior? It would be appallingly dark. The time-honored arrival of Jesus Christ is the most captivating story ever told. This story is written on the Bible's pages and in the hearts of those who believe. Though the news is good because God is good, there are challenges in bringing this idea into our everyday thinking and practice.

Unfortunately, some have flipped the script on the news being good by placing too much emphasis on bad elements they believe are essential for the good news to be heard and received. The reasoning goes something like this: Tell people how terribly sinful, how irretrievably lost, and utterly broken they are. Then hit them with the good news that Jesus saves, and presto, you supposedly have a genuine convert! This approach is deemed necessary because people must understand what they are being saved from. Preaching sinfulness strongly, asserting that goodness can only be appreciated in contrast to what is sinful, bad, and immoral, is how this mindset works. Flipping the script on good news has a chilling effect on people, often leading to confusion and low self-worth.

To illustrate the bad news brand of thinking further, suppose you have a low-interest loan on your home, say about 3%, which is very reasonable in any mortgage market. What if someone advised you to refinance your home with an 8% loan to motivate you to work harder? Bringing about more incredible wealth in the long run because complacency kills and the additional burden will drive you to higher levels of financial achievement. Thus, you become a better wealth manager. We all agree that the aforementioned refinancing scenario is ridiculously ill-advised and financially absurd. Not to mention borderline self-abuse and victimization. But I'm afraid this is the face some put on God. Instead of embracing the good news and accepting grace, a pain-inflicting, hard-nosed version of God is chosen. This mindset establishes a dualism between a God that is sometimes benevolent and occasionally malevolent, depending on what is required to fix humanity. In other words, mandatory hardships and necessary evils are essential to life's journey and should be accepted as part of God working all things together for purportedly good outcomes. In a manner of speaking, God has to do evil so that good may result essentially.

The beginning point of human history offers a different perspective on life. In the beginning, God created the heavens and the earth and declared it was "good" (Genesis 1). Everything that God does is good because goodness and love are the essence of God's being. The first couple, Adam and Eve, experienced all that was good in God's creation. God's goodness preceded Adam and Eve's moral failings in the Genesis narrative. Fast forward to the time of Christ, God didn't suddenly decide to get back on the goodness track in sending Jesus to earth; God's good nature was evident from the dawn of creation. God doesn't need evil to stand in contrast to what is good in order to make it more attractive. Good can be good without evil. An imaginary seesaw in heaven balancing the scales between good and evil is likely not one of God's methods of operation. God is, always has been, and always will be good. God is essentially goodness itself, and the being from which all good things come.

In all its various forms, bad news thinking is still a thing. A few years ago, I nurtured a relationship with a young man struggling to understand the Christian message. With a pre-existing antagonistic attitude toward the Christian faith, he encountered a street evangelist shouting, "Repent, for the kingdom of heaven is at hand." Instead of being attracted to Christianity, he was further repelled. An angry tone and a self-righteous attitude accompanying the word "repent" worsened his impression. The street evangelist failed to portray God in the manner of good news. What kind of God angrily shouts at people? When we think of the Gospel (Good News), we are immediately confronted with questions about the nature and character of God. Confounded by this encounter, his perception of Christianity grew increasingly negative, and therefore, he was inclined to dismiss both the messenger and the message, effectively rejecting God on a totally false premise. Far too often, the Church and its preachers go overboard trying to convince people they are sinners, as if people are somehow unaware of their brokenness. Or, they hyper-focus on some negative aspect of life to create a sense of urgency for people to turn to God. But what if that urgency were God's unrelenting beauty and unsurpassed goodness? How might that be more impacting?

People sharing the good news are who we might call "good newsers." Instead of doom and gloom, good newsers rise to the occasion, announcing the goodness and beauty of God. Does a good newser gloss over challenging aspects of the gospel that call for confession and repentance? No! Messengers of the good news walk a fine line, calling men and women to faith in God while helping them identify areas of their life Christ's transforming power can address. The proper framework for this activity is relationships built on the foundation of love. A good newser crafts a message in a manner consistent with the Bible, declaring God's infinite goodness. From there, the brokenness of humanity is addressed and restoration is realized through the ongoing redemptive activity of God's Spirit. Too much emphasis on humanity's sinful condition and God's judgment leads people to the wrong view of God. It also sets people on the trajectory of focusing on their problems instead of the solution. The looming threat of hell and the pending execution of sinners is not good news.

Let's return to our street preaching example for a moment. Experience teaches us that even when people respond to condemnation preaching, they rarely mature beyond spiritual infancy. The rate of suicide and depression in modern society are solid indicators that people are cognizant of their broken condition already. More than we know, people fundamentally acknowledge their need for God, and some have lived such hard lives that it's as though they have been to a living hell. The good news doesn't become "gooder" when we sin-shame people into belief using fear and condemnation. Clearly communicating God's loving nature—our goal—is far more attractive and compelling, yielding a greater harvest of souls while producing lasting results. Presenting bad news as good news for the purpose of religious conversion confuses people with doubts about whether or not God is in pursuit of their best interests. Good news messaging shows much greater concern for people without the baggage of trying to explain God's meanness seemingly aimed at people who inherently possess such bad qualities that death is warranted. With renewed vision, we can effectively convey the message that God is good all the time, and all the time, God is good!

Good news is why Jesus came to earth. Prominently featured in another story of great beginnings, good news is found in the first recorded gospel attributed to an author named Mark. Chapter one, verse one sets the tone for Mark's gospel story, *"The beginning of the good news about Jesus the Messiah"* (Mark 1: 1). The gospel of Mark is good news for people living in bad times. Mark gives his readers a compelling description of Jesus as the visible representation of God. Accordingly, if we want to know what God is like, reading Mark's gospel through the lens of Mark 1:1

is an excellent starting point. Jesus embodies the exponential goodness of God in this beloved narrative. The great beginnings in the Bible are marinated in God's goodness, clearly indicating how we should think, live, and be.

I am living proof that the face of God is good news. If not for God's goodness and the saving activity of Jesus Christ, I'm pretty sure I would have hit the eject button and left for eternity at an earlier stage of my life. People who do not have anything to live for, in a good sense, tend to live in despair, missing out on the fullness of life. An increasingly clear view of God's nature and character is needed to save lives, and yes, the matter is that urgent. As we deepen our awareness of God's goodness, I trust fewer people will want to hit the eject button. In far too many segments of society and the church, God is portrayed as a "bad newser," and bad news condemnation preachers produce dispirited people who not only leave the faith but also want to quit life altogether. The message of good news dismantles the darkness surrounding God's character, replacing it with life-giving hope. If there is bad news to bear, and there is, that news is a commentary on humanity's condition and the cruel nature of sin and evil in our world. But don't stay there; we must move on to a solutions-based message!

Good news is vital to embrace and good newsers share in the nature of God. Imitating God's goodness is the primary function of a good newser. Imitating God may sound a bit crazy, but it is something people of the Christian faith have aspired to for centuries. According to the Apostle Paul, it is our duty and sacred calling, *"Therefore **be imitators of God**, as beloved children; and walk in love, just as Christ also loved you and gave Himself up for us"* (Ephesians 5: 1-2). I recently painted a portion of this verse on a slab of wood. I wanted to have a visible reminder and hang it on my wall. Good newsers imitate God as they share in the nature of God's being. God invites us into goodness, and we become that goodness. A good newser internalizes God's nature while outwardly reflecting those values. As we become more like God, the news we dispense and our whole way of life become increasingly good, leaving fewer opportunities for negativity to grip our souls.

Many years ago, a sermon infamously titled, *"Sinners in the hands of an angry God,"* delivered by a preacher named Jonathan Edwards, stirred the hearts of many. During the Great Awakening in the early 1700s, sermons depicting God's wrath were standard. Edward's hell-fire sermon rippled through the audience as he invoked terrifying images of people dangling over the great furnace of God's wrath by a slender thread until they repented of their sins. The notion of God's razor-thin patience unfurled on people without an ounce of pity took hold. Edward's famous sermon struck fear in the hearts of listeners and people responded with tears of confession and cries for mercy. They felt they had no other choice but to run to God or be damned to hell's flames. It was bad news preaching on steroids: Sin is bad and God is madder than hell.

No sermon has impacted America's religious landscape more than this one and not for the better. Is God really that angry? I don't think so. Terrorizing people for their sins, ridiculing their vices, exploiting their temptations, etc. Is all of that necessary to produce life transformation? Not according to my interpretation of the Bible. I think Edwards failed in his duties as a preacher. In good faith, he did bad theology. He promoted an angry perception of God. If God is the heartless being Edwards claims, nobody stands a chance, not even Edwards. Who could stand before this God? Not. One. Single. Human.

The face of good news lies in the portrayal of a God eager to offer salvation rather than condemnation. Instead of preaching "Sinners in the hands of an angry God," a more accurate depiction would be "Sinners cradled in the hands of a merciful and loving God." Edward's renowned sermon was an adventure in missing the point because God's fundamental disposition towards humanity is one of love and mercy, not retribution and judgment. If God's nature were anything but merciful, despair would overshadow hope, rendering existence futile and masses would scramble to hit the eject button. How is that even possible when every glimpse of beauty in the world, from the innocence of a newborn's face to the warmth of the morning sun and the majesty of crashing waves reflects an infinity of goodness? Life's goodness is a testament to a God who loves us unconditionally, not one who needs anger therapy. Ultimately, the greatness of love, not the looming threat of hell, draws us towards repentance. As stated in Romans 2:4, it is God's kindness that turns our hearts back to Him. God's kindness in sending Christ is good news, declaring unconditional love, acceptance, and forgiveness, not fear, judgment, and wrath.

A focus on the goodness nature of God supports improved mental health. Although I lack clinical data to prove this directly, I'm confident I could assemble a wealth of personal testimonies as evidence to support my thesis. Aggressive views of God tend to heighten anxieties, creating a sense of despair rather than hope. When we think this way, our perception of God's goodness becomes limited, leaving us anxious about the future and suspicious of those who hold different beliefs. This mindset often leads to stress, spiritual disillusionment, and human conflict. In contrast, a theology grounded in good news cultivates hope and optimism, reminding us that God's vast goodness surpasses any narrow view. If poor theology can negatively impact mental health, then surely good theology has the opposite effect. Do people who focus on God's goodness experience improved mental health? I believe so. When we embrace God's goodness, we open ourselves to a deeper, more fulfilling connection with Him, which naturally promotes a healthier mindset.

The face of good news is a vital component of spiritual health in Christian community. When religious groups over-emphasize things like judgment, God's wrath, the apocalypse, etc., it often stems from an underlying element of insecurity or lack of true faith. These insecurities breed fears and quests for control, paving the way for authoritarian behavior and spiritual harm. Human beings behave poorly toward one another when they operate with bad theology. Good newsers, however, take a different path. Instead of retreating to the dark psychology of God's judgment and wrath, good news faith communities nurture confidence in a God who has overcome the world, triumphing over evil with good. Communities that organize around good news values stand firm against debilitating insecurities, drawing strength from humility rather than positions of control and authority. I hope you are part of a good news community. If so, you should be witnessing high levels of treatment toward other human beings and enjoying fellowship with people committed to the endeavor of displaying God's goodness. If you are not currently connected with a good news community, it's never too late to find one that aspires to live by these values.

In this chapter, we've surveyed the various ways in which good news is tied to God's nature and helps us experience the fullness of life. We've also discussed the downsides of yielding to the dark psychology of God's judgment and wrath purportedly unleashed on sinners. Excessive focus on humanity's broken state while neglecting God's overcoming grace has a paralyzing effect on our spiritual welfare. The key to living a good life, even a great one, is closely related to finding solutions and progressing toward good outcomes. This is why I advocate for spreading the universal message of God's good news through the person of Jesus Christ, who fully embodied the attributes of God's character. When we look at Jesus, we see the face of God and all that is good in life.

Spiritual Formation

- Are you a good newser? How does your life reflect God's goodness?

- Have you ever seen a preacher or church take things too far in trying to convince people they're living in sin? Have you ever encountered a condemnation preacher?

- Read Genesis Chapter 1 and Mark Chapter 1; what do they have in common? How do these stories each proclaim the goodness nature of God?

- Do you have negative people in your life who live with a defeatist mentality? How does a good newser respond? What steps will you take to ensure the good news is heard?

- Far too many people live in a state of depression and anxiety, wanting to hit the eject button and exit life.

How can the spiritual health of a faith community be a life-saving station for these people?

- What good news steps can you take today? Who will you encourage? How will you enact the positive life values that flow from sharing in God's nature?

- More than just "good vibes," good news is a powerful revelation, unveiling the work of a Savior in our hearts. Create a journal entry that explores the benefits of being a good newser and how embracing the good news facilitates the fullness of life.

Chapter Four
The face of God when I face my emotions

> *Triple Prayer: "O most merciful Redeemer, Friend, and Brother, of you three things I pray: To see you more clearly, love you more dearly, follow you more nearly, day by day."*
> —*Richard of Chichester (1197–1253)*

How often have you hidden your emotions, fearing they might be dismissed? This is a common struggle in our relationship with God and others. What you feel is essential to who you are as a human being, and those feelings deserve validation. God does that, but when people tell us to get over it, we suppress what we feel, forming a pattern of avoidance. Sometimes used as a survival mechanism, avoidance tactics protect us from people who might weaponize those feelings and emotions against us. Human feelings are complex, and you won't find detailed explanations here about why we feel the way we do about ourselves, God, or others. I'm not writing as someone who has it all figured out—our emotions are intricate, subjective, and deeply personal. Like trying to untangle a knotted ball of yarn, our feelings and emotions are not easily unraveled. There is, however, a starting point from which we can begin a conversation that might produce some answers. God is that starting point.

Starting with God stands in stark contrast to popular psychological methods. Humanistic psychology, a perspective that emerged in the mid-20th century, places human experience at the nucleus of understanding. While human experience is important, we may be at a loss for answers to some of life's biggest questions if we rely on human experience alone. I believe that humans need God-oriented ways of addressing questions like: *Why am I here? Who am I? Why do I feel the way I do?* The humanistic psychology approach does not yield satisfying answers and the importance of issues like self-worth, the reason for living, and relationships with others demand spiritual inquiry with God. What if we were to begin with the creator and not the creation?

Think about the possibilities. Rather than diving deeper into yourself, with all due respect to the field of psychology, consider a deeper discovery of God. As a tool of understanding, behavioral science has much to offer when it comes to the vastness of human emotions. But there is a wealth of insight to be gained from starting a conversation with God about our feelings because life itself is rooted in a God who knows our innermost parts.

The story of a young man who saw God is told in the Old Testament. His name is Isaiah. His vision of God is a bit of a mystery; we're unsure if it was a dream or a spiritual epiphany. We know where it occurred: Isaiah caught a glimpse of God's majestic holiness while worshipping in the Jerusalem temple. Upon seeing the brilliance of God,

Isaiah responded with confession because he saw things within himself that needed to change. He begged God to touch his soul with forgiveness and purity. God delivered and Isaiah's life was indeed touched. You can read about Isaiah's dramatic experience seeing God in the book that bears his name (Isaiah 6).

What can we learn from Isaiah's encounter? One possible lesson is where the journey began. A solid assessment of oneself begins with God. Isaiah's vision of God became the lens through which he could see his inner life more accurately. In seeing God, self-examination came to fruition, bringing humble confession and life transformation. Isaiah's unguarded moment of confession also became the catalyst for a higher life calling. From there, he accepted God's invitation to work among a nation of people desperately needing spiritual leadership. The experience altered the trajectory of Isaiah's life because nothing changes us more than gazing upon God's face. For Isaiah, a clear vision of God was the starting point in determining his spiritual state and personal identity.

A current trend of the age is self-fulfillment and enlightenment from within. Once again, humanistic psychology's approach is to begin with the person and not God, which can quickly lead to self-worship. I contend that starting with God offers a better path, even though counterarguments to this suggestion are strong. Which God? Some will argue. The God of past wars? The God who created evil? The God who condemns sinners? To which I respond: do these versions of God even exist? What if they are only caricatures and false perceptions? The critical work of challenging our assumptions about God is a task we should all undertake. That said, a theology test in the afterlife isn't likely, so it is entirely possible to miss the mark theologically and not jeopardize your soul. I suppose many of us fit into that category, but if we have the opportunity—and we do—we should strive to better understand God and sharpen our spiritual vision. Isaiah's dramatic self-revelation began with God, and we would benefit from adopting that same starting point. Looking inward isn't something we should necessarily avoid; it is best done in partnership with God, who illuminates the true condition of our soul from which all our feelings and emotions are derived.

Beginning with God is consistent with the first phrase of the famous Triple Prayer quoted at the outset of this chapter: *To see God more clearly*. The journey from who you are to who you can become begins and ends with a God eager to disclose everything you need to know for heightened self-awareness, continued growth, and Christ-like maturity. The proper starting point in any journey is the key to progress, and a sharper vision of God gives us a much-needed introspective advantage. Who we are and who we can become is determined by who God is. Human beings tend to reflect the likeness of the God they worship.

Let's return to our pesky feelings, especially the unpleasant ones. Too often, well-intentioned religious teachers teach the concept of putting faith over feelings. While this idea has some merit, it also has some severe pitfalls because it can lead to two possible outcomes, both of which are harmful: 1) A God who devalues human emotions and doesn't want to be bothered with them; in other words, unsympathetic. 2) An individual who neglects what is happening internally through some form of feeling suppression. Teaching people that faith should triumph over feelings requires proper qualifications and a fair amount of caution. Using religion and spirituality to bypass unresolved emotional issues is one of those cautions. Conversely, we must be careful not to venture down the path of allowing feelings and emotions to reign over every aspect of our faith development. I like to say my faith has feelings and even with my best intentions, I may not always get them right.

We've already established God as a starting point, allowing us to assess ourselves and discern feelings and emotions. Even so, I suspect the amount of feelings and emotions that people actually pour out to God is small due to condemnation fears. This is why we all stand to benefit from adopting a framework of love. Love, which by definition, is empathetic and sympathetic. We can safely assume a God of love is genuinely interested in the well-being of people like you and me because God became a human and experienced the fullness of humanity. According to 1 John 4:8, God's chief attribute is love, and not only is God love, but God works by love in all of God's dealings. With that idea firmly in place, we can be assured the magnitude and intensity of our feelings enjoy a sympathetic and empathetic reception. Unfortunately, unsympathetic versions of God flood our minds, making us think we shouldn't bother God with all those complicated feelings and emotions because God isn't interested, and God has never felt pain on the level of humans. Those versions of God cripple us on our spiritual journey.

Even within the framework of love, a certain amount of fear creeps in that must be dealt with. Some important reminders are in order. According to the Scriptures, there is no fear in love, but that doesn't mean we won't struggle (Ephesians 5:1-2). Being afraid to identify and bring our feelings before God is a natural human response, especially when those feelings are unpleasant and uncomfortable. Thankfully, God doesn't operate in the realm of fear and God's love extends to the whole person. Despite what we may be feeling, God's faithful love is ready to assist us in dissolving the fears that hold us back. In that sense, there is nothing to fear but fear itself—to borrow a famous line.

In my spiritual work with men, dealing with emotions is a big issue because male stereotypes get in the way. Social conditioning, harmful religious instruction, and malformed views of God influence men wrongly. The stiff upper lip of manhood and personal pride represent some of the battles persistently fought within the masculine domain, often leading to male posing. A poser externally presents one version of themselves to people in public, that of a tough guy, while being something entirely different in private. Fears of being perceived as weak-minded and less manly fuel the poser mindset, leading many men into a trap. The facade crumbles when those feelings and emotions seep out in relationally destructive ways, which is often the case with posing men.

I've experienced this firsthand. Rather than embracing vulnerability in following God, I've fallen prey to male stereotypes and perceptions of God that are unsympathetic. This approach never ends well, as it fosters self-protectionism and emotional distancing. The escape from this guarded state is envisioning a God whose love surpasses our egos and emotions. A sympathetic God who has emotions and understands them can be trusted to carry ours. With a clearer vision of God, pathways to our inner lives open up, replacing guarded silence—akin to a masculine tombstone—with Christ-like maturity.

A piece of excellent advice about feelings came to me through a wise mentor who said every feeling deserves to be felt, but not every feeling deserves to be followed. That statement resonated deeply in my soul and helped me think about how God responds to us. A sympathetic God validates my feelings while gently nudging me not to follow certain feelings. What a refreshing perspective! Sorting through a range of feelings and emotions I would otherwise have suppressed suddenly felt more liberating. I've learned that it is okay to feel what I am feeling, and those feelings supply the motivational energy necessary for change. But it's not advisable to follow certain feelings, especially ones leading to jealousy, hatred of others, or some other form of brokenness. The possibility that some of our feelings are built on an entirely false premise is also very real. Yet, a God of unlimited love responds sympathetically to the whole person, including those awkward moments in life when our feelings get too big and human emotions threaten to overpower us. A sympathetic God is patient and understanding, not scornful and angry toward us for being human. We live our lives through our emotions and should be able to do this without fear of condemnation. Nearly every human emotion can be healthily expressed to God.

In today's world, many people benefit from the help of therapists, counselors, life coaches, and mentors. I applaud the move, especially when it is done in conjunction with a God who loves. It's possible to utilize the best the field of psychology offers while heeding the upward call of seeing God as our creator, comforter, and counselor. Not everyone struggling in life will have access to these wonderful resources, but everyone has access to a God who loves and the Spirit of God who consoles. The face of God brimming with empathy and understanding is a hope I pray many will discover.

To the one reading this who feels like you're on the verge of giving up, I want to encourage you to take another look at God. "Look and live" as a spiritual principle emerged from the Old Testament, where Moses set up a bronze serpent in the wilderness. In times of distress, the Israelites were instructed to gaze upon this object as a symbol of mercy and healing (Numbers 21: 4-9). Later, Jesus used this reference as an object lesson to describe His ministry, *"Just as Moses lifted up the snake in the wilderness, so the Son of Man must be lifted up, that everyone who believes may have eternal life in him." For God so loved the world that he gave his one and only Son, that whoever believes in him shall not perish but have eternal life"* (John 3: 14-16).

The message is clear: Look and live. Just as gazing upon a brass serpent in the wilderness brought healing, so does looking upon Jesus, the face of an invisible God and the perfect representation of all that is truly human. No matter where you find yourself today or your emotional state, consider taking one more look at God. Self-fulfillment gurus and humanistic psychology often overlook the impact of defining oneself in light of God. Looking to God helps us avoid all the pitfalls of becoming the center of our own universe. Transformation through a new vision of God could be the change you seek. If you urgently need encouragement, skip to Chapter 11, which focuses on the shining face of God, and start reading.

Spiritual Formation

- Complete a journal entry that takes stock of your feelings.

    A few examples of feelings and emotions: anxious, indifferent, miserable, satisfied, surprised, lonely, angry, puzzled, joyful, curious, happy, sad, perplexed, thoughtful, sympathetic, fearful, loving, jealous, confused, caring, disappointed, kind, cherished, thankful, other:_____

- How would I benefit from registering these feelings with God? What are your reasons for holding back?

- How do I feel about God? Choose from the feelings in the list above or add others that come to mind when you reflect on your perception of God.

- What face do I put on God that prevents me from facing my true feelings?

- An empathetic God invites us to register feelings without following certain feelings. How does that advice help you process big feelings and strong emotions?

- Exercise: Read Psalm 63, written by David, a shepherd turned king of the Israelites, who had learned to view God relationally as well as holy and worthy of awe. Write down any words or phrases describing how David viewed God.

- The face of God shows curiosity and empathy toward our feelings, not condemnation. How might that way of seeing God inform your response to people you have a relationship with?

- Looking and living as a spiritual principle has much to offer. Seeing the face of an invisible God in Jesus brings a refreshing amount of hope. Is this a new concept for you? How might looking and living become a useful self-reflection tool on your spiritual journey?

Chapter Five
The face of a partnering God

*For we are co-workers in God's service; you are God's field,
God's building. -1 Corinthians 3: 9*

Heroic acts, mystical power waves, and surprise interventions characterize how some view God. "My God can do anything," they say. To borrow the refrain from a popular children's hymn, "My God is so big, so strong and so mighty, there is nothing my God cannot do!" A hero God coming to our rescue sounds impressive, and as an idea, it has some validity, but some questions need to be answered. Can God heroically step into our lives at any moment according to our faith and sometimes, despite our faith? The heroic version of God poses several problems, the most concerning of which is how it undermines our partnership with God. A God of heroic quality is rarely questioned: If God is God, anything can be accomplished, right?

"I just want God to take it away," said Thomas, a struggling alcoholic. "Every time I see a beer commercial on TV or an ad for alcohol on a billboard, my brain goes haywire trying to pursue it." Thomas, and many like him struggling with addiction, imagine God stepping in and removing the problem completely. Appetite destruction is their plea. The outright cancellation of a vice is their hope. God rarely, if ever, works that way. Why not? Some may wonder. Why shouldn't God intervene on behalf of an addict with miraculous deliverance, setting that person free once and for all? Thousands of lives could be saved, people would flock to God, and the world would be better. Addiction freedom is undoubtedly desirable, but getting there isn't that easy.

Do we really want a Hero-God zapping people out of their troubles at the expense of free will? Does God perform mighty acts without human consent and cooperation? Challenging questions to ponder. The hero version of God diminishes our standing by reducing the role of humans to mere onlookers. Minimizing human participation is inconsistent with God's character and vision for humanity. God's beauty and brilliance are not always seen in heroic acts but in meaningful human engagement through partnering relationships that bear witness to a synergy of forces.

Indeed, God performs heroic acts in the Bible, and we might even say that history records such events; however, divine acts that do not involve cooperative humans are pretty scarce. Instead, engaged partnerships over longer passages of time appear to be the norm. Old Testament examples include David, Moses, and Joseph. Long-term actions through people who partner with God are the typical pattern, not sudden interventions. The lone hero version of God is mostly, if not entirely, inaccurate. The true face of God is one of continuous partnership over time. Let me explain why the hero version of God hinders instead of helps and how a partnering version of God offers something better.

First, heroic God-thinking is deceitful because it fuels unrealistic expectations. Praying for God to do things that God cannot or will not necessarily do isn't a new phenomenon. Throughout history, people have frequently prayed for divine intervention in matters such as the healing of loved ones, agricultural blessings like rain for crops, or triumph in conflicts. Often, these prayers are not answered in the manner requested. Discrepancies between human desires and God's ways are documented in various biblical accounts. We sometimes want God to act in ways inconsistent with who God is. A genie in a bottle, an idol, or a God of instant gratification are faces we subconsciously put on God without realizing these expectations reduce God to a being we can manipulate.

Christians are right to ponder God's abilities, inabilities, and willingness to act heroically in light of their own experiences. It's a meaningful conversation to be had with God and with other faithful believers. To be clear, when a person emphasizes God's ability to act heroically, with or without human instruments, it can be a set up for grave disappointment. It is also a possible growth opportunity that could be missed. Let me give an example.

A minister's daughter fell terribly ill, and the prognosis was grim. The disease from which she suffered is not one a small child typically survives. The call went out for prayer, and people responded en masse. Fervent intercession stormed the gates of heaven. Faith healing services were held, and people believed in the child's total restoration. "We don't care what the doctors say; we have God," they proclaimed. Despite their prayers, the child's illness progressed. Shock and disappointment came when the child passed, and then rationalizations began. "God needed another angel" was the word. The pendulum swung from miraculous healing to heavenly child abduction. How did God get to be like that?

Are people of zealous faith wrong to ask God for healing? No. It only becomes problematic when the level of expectation for heroic action runs off the charts. Unfortunately, thousands of children die of sickness and disease in the world daily. Human mortality is a relentless foe. Well-intentioned people praying for God to heroically act against all odds with the expectation it will happen because they want it to is not realistic, especially when those prayers marginalize medical care. This kind of thinking can also short-circuit healthy grieving. There's a path forward that tempers expectations without clinging to a view of God that devastates people with unfulfilled hopes. Partnering with God in both life and death is that path.

A healthy view of God accounts for untimely deaths and human suffering, seeing them as opportunities to awaken our lives to resurrection hope. God's grand promises to conquer death with life unfold in ways that may diverge from our immediate expectations. Thus, we find ourselves situated in the "not yet" phase of God's overarching plan to renew and restore creation to its fullness. If we could only grasp the bigger picture, our lives would be spared the deceit of thinking God will heroically replace our present sufferings with trouble-free living.

Secondly, heroic God-thinking is disillusioning. Instead of deepening our faith, it actually achieves the opposite. Mature faith evolves as we navigate through periods of pain and suffering, not solely because we are miraculously rescued from them. Disillusionment of faith occurs when we think God should rescue us from a situation we are not rescued from, causing us to wonder: "Are you afflicting me with pain on purpose, Lord?" "Did I do something wrong?" The formation of faith, however, is more often seen when we experience what one biblical author describes as *"trials of many kinds"* (James 1:2). Adopting the heroic God mindset predisposes us to a feeling of entitlement when it comes to being rescued from life's hardships, when, in fact, we may benefit from learning from those hardships.

Take Riley, for example. She accumulated enormous financial debt from a failed business venture. She listens to prosperity preachers who insist God's children are destined for wealthy living. "God owns the cattle on a thousand hills," they claim in their sermons. In other words, if you have faith, pray, and tithe your income, you're entitled to wealth because your faith appropriates the riches of heaven. Unfortunately, things didn't work out, and Riley's business failed. She feels misled and her version of God has let her down.

Why didn't God save the business and grant her success? She did all the prescribed things, like paying her tithe and holding out for a miracle. Riley threw the towel in on God out of frustration. Her faulty perception of God came crashing down, leaving her disappointed and angry. *Can God ever be trusted?* She keeps asking herself. Certainly not her version of God. Riley must now heal from what I call heroic God trauma. She was manipulated into a system of belief with unrealistic promises. Poor religious instruction, wild ambition, and sky-high human expectations were some of the forces at work in the demise of her fragile faith. Expecting God to do things God cannot necessarily do is disillusioning. Where does Riley go from here? It will take time, but a new partnership with God can be forged if she is willing.

Thirdly, heroic God-thinking is dumbfounding because it minimizes human participation. The invitation to journey with God requires full participation. God does God's best work in partnership with humans. Mystical power waves, heroic acts, and surprise interventions fail to engage humans in deep relationships. God is interested in participation, not entertainment or appeasement. Participation emboldens human development and invigorates faith. A partnering God empowers human responsibility instead of minimizing it. When it comes to solving some of life's biggest problems, God works in us, through us, and with us. A brilliant union between God and God's creatures built on a foundation of mutual love: A team of co-laborers collaborating in the work of creation. Without collaboration, human motivation would fizzle. People would sit around and wait for God to be Superman and they would miss the beauty of co-creating with God.

A roller coaster of highs and lows, elations and sorrows flow from the expectation that God will perform mind-blowing heroic acts on our behalf. Our emotional state wavers when those expectations change or God doesn't deliver in the manner of our thinking. Grounding our faith in a partnering version of God is the stabilizing solution. A faith-filled heart in conjunction with God-inspired human action has biblical support: *"Faith without works is dead,"* says James 2:26. This can also be translated as *"faith without corresponding action is dead."* Real faith is defined by a willingness to join God in what God is doing. Really good things, miraculous things, I would say, happen when we put our faith to work.

"You have to give God something to work with," said an old Southern preacher. That's participation! Working with God in partnership trumps the high-flying expectations of a Hero-God saving the day. However, God does save the day more than we may know because God actively partners with other willing heroes, even when those heroes don't profess faith. God is at work despite our lack of awareness and willingness. Other cooperating agents are found and God's work marches on. This is why we should awaken ourselves daily to the work of God that is taking place and actively partner with God in making the world a more wholesome place to live. With God, we have the sacred honor of creating a new reality for ourselves and others. This is the synergy that cures boredom and keeps humans engaged in hopeful living.

The face of a partnering God has been an enormous blessing in my life. I have learned and am still learning how to cooperate with God to reflect good outcomes. In 2020, I was infected with the COVID-19 virus. Initially, I did not think it would linger, but it did. A year and a half later, I contracted the virus again, and like the previous infection, the symptoms lingered. My body's immune response left me with fatigue and brain fog for several months. Hoping to return to health, I sought treatment. I prayed, I took prescribed medicine, I altered my diet, and I reduced stress. I did everything under the sun to regain my pre-COVID strength and well-being. In moments of desperation, I cried out, "This is terrible! Lord, make it go away!" The prayer was not immediately answered; in fact, things got worse, and I suffered from a third infection of COVID-19 in 2023. This time, a newly approved therapeutic drug expedited my recovery. The long road back to health was a journey marked by many challenges and setbacks from which I learned patience, perseverance, and empathy for other sufferers. The results were far from instantaneous. It was more like a marathon that involved trusting God, working with physicians, relying on prescribed therapies and treatments, and praying they would be effective.

God desires our cooperation, and we can live our best life when we consent to labor with God. Expecting God to mystically appear, suddenly intervene, and miraculously move, in many instances, skirts human responsibility. But when we give God something to work with, striking the right balance between faith and works, new dimensions of living are possible. God is not a solo act. The very nature of the triune Godhead reveals community. God relishes engagement with other members of the Trinity, the world, and human creatures. Will you cooperate with God fully? I call this version of God post-heroic. The post-heroic version of God invites cooperation, collaboration, community, faith, action, and perseverance. This is the God I have come to know and love—a God who does not act unilaterally in a way that reduces humans to mere bystanders.

For application purposes, let's take it a step further. Prayer is where most of our theology is put to the test. How do heroic and post-heroic views of God hold up? To the person overwhelmed with escalating financial debt, instead of praying, "Lord, erase my indebtedness," pray, "Lord, help me make wise financial decisions that will allow full payment to my creditors." To the person battling addiction, instead of praying, "Lord, cancel my addictive behaviors," pray, "Lord, guide my recovery, and with your help and the skill of experts, I can live victoriously." To the person struggling with an abusive relationship, instead of praying, "Lord, zap this person out of my life," pray, "Lord, what are you teaching me about healthy boundaries and relationships?"

The face of a partnering God is beautiful in every way because it raises the ceiling on what is possible in this life. Good things happen more frequently when we work with God to create outcomes that align with God's character. Remember the story of the prophet Isaiah from an earlier chapter? Isaiah's lifelong partnership with God began when *"Isaiah saw the Lord..."* (Isaiah 6:1). His corresponding response, *"Here am I, send me"* was the beginning of a new adventure (Isaiah 6:8). Isaiah seized God's partnership invitation and that's my prayer for you today. God is inviting you into a bigger story. You and God can make history together. Partnership with God is your destiny. Will you say yes?

Some readers may get the impression that I am stripping God of power. Objections to the idea that God is anything less than heroic will be raised. The pushback is expected. People share stories and give testimony to God's mighty acts in healing a family member from cancer or saving someone's life. I am not dismissive of those claims, and rest assured God is heroic in the sense God's saving work is one hundred percent in play where human effort leaves off. Humanity's redemption depends upon the idea of God doing something for us we could not do for ourselves (Ephesians 2: 8-9).

The face of a partnering God goes beyond that idea to the everyday minutia of life where most faith living occurs. Chasing the next surprise intervention, heroic act, or mystical power wave isn't a healthy life path, especially when human participation is minimized. This concept is hard for many folks because they have been taught to doubt human effort. They worry God will not accept their involvement or that their efforts will somehow be construed as merit to earn salvation. Yet, we bear the image of our creator, and we all possess some degree of inherent goodness and natural capability to create. Engaging in a creative partnership amplifies God's true nature in our lives. God loves inviting us into creative life endeavors; it is the purpose for which we were made.

Our conversation here represents a lens through which we can interpret God's activity in our lives. It's not the final word; much more could be written, studied, and shared. My plea is for patience; we are all learning, growing, and sharpening our ability to convey a better vision of God. If you are committed to partnering with God, welcome to a lifetime journey of discovery. And you will probably see more of what some call everyday "miracles!"

Spiritual Formation

- When you see God, do you see the face of a partnering God who values your input and invites your participation? Journal your thoughts. Identify times in which you have relied on a heroic version of God. What happened? What did you learn? Also, identify the times in your life when you put your faith to work to achieve good outcomes. How did your partnership with God benefit others and achieve success?

- Imagine Riley seeking spiritual advice, and you are in a position to advise her. What would you tell her about God that might help her live more meaningfully through the disappointment of a failed business venture?

- As you reflect on life hardships, how did you benefit from going through them instead of escaping them?

Were you tempted to utilize escape tactics? How did your faith grow?

- React to the statement, "You and God can make history together." What does it look like for you? What dreams might unfold as you co-create the future together with God?

Chapter Six
The face of God bleeds mercy

*The Lord is gracious and merciful, slow to anger
and abounding in steadfast love.*
-Psalm 145:8

In an earlier chapter, I describe God-blurring and various influences in our lives that obscure our perception of God. We all come into this world as a blank slate, and over time, our view of God is shaped for good or ill. Inevitably, some of those influences will distort God's image and blur understandings surrounding God's true character. Blurring activity is rarely intentional and malicious. It isn't done on purpose. In good faith, people do bad theology. *How is this overcome?* You might ask. *Does anyone get it right?* The answers are found in the bleed. Let me explain.

Blood stains are a nightmare. A scraped knee, a bloody nose, or whatever injury breaks your skin will likely produce a potent red stain on clothing, bandaging, carpet, etc. Bright red stains turn to a darker hue after oxygen exposure and can be very hard to remove. Putting water on a blood stain can accelerate the spread. Blood potency runs right through the fabric. It's impossible to go through life without breaking your skin and bleeding out to the point you need to be bandaged. Years ago, I had major reconstructive surgery performed on my foot. Surgeons applied an astounding amount of bandaging to the surgical site. I didn't think my sewn-up wounds would bleed through those layers of bandages, but indeed, the blood found a way. The next time you prick your finger, let one drop of blood fall into a sink basin filled with water. Within seconds, it will taint every visible ounce of available water with a tinge of pink.

God's mercy stains like blood. It bleeds through our lives from beginning to end, marking us with goodness and the potency of this goodness we cannot escape. No life on planet Earth is void of God's mercy due to its pervasiveness over time and eternity. The bleed of God's mercy runs deep through the history of all civilizations, bringing us to the present moment. Whether that mercy is seen or unseen, recognized or not, is a matter of perspective. In my theological understanding, it begs for attention and compels us to explore. The vast majority of the human race may not acknowledge the goodness and mercy of God, but that does not make it any less prevalent in our lives.

I assume you are interested in exploration because you are reading a book about putting a new face on God. We previously identified cruel versions of God frequently appearing in the Old Testament portion of the Bible (Chapter 2: The Face of a Cruel God). Troubling biblical accounts raise questions about God's reputation as a bloodthirsty tyrant. But isn't there more to the story? What about references to God's mercy and kindness? Accounts of God's goodness are plentiful. A better version of God unfolds in forward-like motion, anticipating Jesus, the ultimate picture of God. Let's go to some of those places.

In the book of beginnings, Genesis, God's merciful hand guides Adam and Eve. The Garden of Eden, presumably the first civilization, was a paradise of sorts. The first couple enjoyed a beautiful life with God under one condition: not to eat from the Tree of Knowledge. But what did Adam and Eve do? The opposite of what God commanded. Now, enter the problem of human shame and guilt. Adam and Eve hid from God as sin's nakedness exposed their disobedient hearts. In the wake of human failure, the writer of Genesis takes great pains to describe God's compassionate response. A beautiful picture of God unfolds, ending those paralyzing moments of sin-induced silence. God not only ended the silence but clothed their naked bodies with animal skins. Accordingly, the God of the Hebrew and Christian scriptures was first known as a God of tender mercy prior to any other recorded revelation. Instead of sin-shaming Adam and Eve, the hands of mercy knit the pelts of animal skins together, covering their skin and, metaphorically speaking, their sin. God's restorative energy is palpable, and while the marks of sin and disobedience change life forever, Adam and Eve's God does not forsake them (see Genesis 3: 21-22).

In another stunning revelation, the book of Deuteronomy describes a society structured around mercy and human dignity. Set in the Stone Age era, Deuteronomy's vision of economic justice elevated orphans, aliens, and widows. It also contained provisions for the ethical treatment of animals! Something I would like to see a lot more of in our day. Perhaps its most significant contribution is the beloved Shema, a prayer to love: *"Hear, O Israel: The LORD our God, the LORD is one. You shall love the LORD your*

God with all your heart and with all your soul and with all your might. And these words that I command you today shall be on your heart." (Deuteronomy 6:4). Loving God and showing mercy to those for whom the system had failed is paramount. Most modern politicians would balk at this brand of governance because its ambitions eclipse budgetary reality. Such things do not bind God's vision; mercy is its own economy, and love for the less fortunate always rises to the top of God's agenda. Despite how we may interpret various passages depicting God's cruelty in the Old Testament, visions like the one found in Deuteronomy trump those accounts with mercy and justice for all.

The book of Jonah provides yet another example of God's endless mercy. Called by God to preach to the Ninevites, Jonah fled in the opposite direction. The Ninevites had a despicable reputation, and Jonah didn't want anything to do with saving them. After fleeing from God and getting swallowed by a whale, Jonah reluctantly agrees to obey God and preach. In preaching to the Ninevites, Jonah witnessed a flood of God's sin-forgiving grace as an entire nation was saved from moral destruction. The story climaxes with Jonah sulking under a tree, consumed with himself instead of the welfare of others. In an angry stupor, Jonah is shattered. God is precisely who he feared God might be: merciful, something he could not outrun.

Once again, mercy bleeds through. Debates about whether a fish literally swallowed Jonah miss the point entirely. The real message of Jonah is God's love for prodigal nations and reluctant prophets who try to escape who God really is. If we drill down further, it is also apparent that neither God nor Jonah saw the fish-swallowing event as punishment. It, too, was an act of mercy, and Jonah's prayer reflects the praiseworthiness of God's saving act,

"But I, with shouts grateful praise, will sacrifice to you. What I have vowed I will make good. I will say, 'Salvation comes from the Lord,'" (Jonah 2:9). The book of Jonah is a tale of God's mercy being told from the deepest of depths and the farthest reaches of human experience. Mercy calls, swallows, and spits, revealing a God of second chances. That's the book of Jonah in a nutshell.

One of the best-known expressions of mercy comes from a minor prophet named Micah. Called by God to prophesy in the southern regions of Israel, Micah's blue-collar brand of preaching hit home. Moving people toward a better relationship with God and others seems to have been Micah's primary focus. The people of Israel, at the time, were spiritually mired down in rituals, sacrifices, and misguided attempts to please God. To correct these problems, Micah made a three-fold suggestion in accordance with his understanding of God, *"He has shown you, O mortal, what is good. And what does the LORD require of you? To act justly and to love mercy and to walk humbly with your God."* Micah 6:8 is the only place where the command to love mercy is given. What does that mean? It means we are called to love what God is. God is mercy, and God loves His own being. Micah's famous verse illuminates the character of God, and his readers are challenged to embrace the attribute of mercy. Loving mercy is not just a command but a way of life. In addition, we are challenged to walk humbly and act justly, characteristics derived from a relationship with a merciful God.

My eleven-year-old dog, Ginger, bleeds mercy. She doesn't have an aggressive bone in her body. Besides chasing a cat or two in her history, she doesn't have a mean streak. Even when she does pursue a cat, it is for the thrill of a chase and not mortal combat. Regarding humans,

Ginger is constantly kind; she loves everyone and has a legendary reputation among our many guests. She has no enemies at all. A painfully short memory is another quality of hers. When Ginger is denied a trip in the car or a walk to the park, she quickly forgives and forgets. I have bad days, but not Ginger; no matter what happens, she wags her tail when I walk in through the door, signaling everything will be okay. Have you ever seen the nature of God reflected in a pet? In a lot of ways, Ginger is like God: constant mercy. God's memory is also short. Sins are promptly forgiven, and offenses are actually forgotten (Micah 7:19). With God, there are no bad days because opportunities for goodness abound. Mercy is who God is and what God does. As an attribute of God, mercy bleeds through the pages of Scripture, eclipsing misunderstandings and misguided perceptions to the contrary.

We recently tested Ginger's temperament by bringing home a rambunctious puppy. As she's been the only dog for many years, we weren't sure how she'd handle the situation. Puppies are full of energy and tend to ignore boundaries, making them a handful. Whether or not we'd adopt this one depended on Ginger's reaction. Based on her history of kindness, I thought she'd be fine, but we needed to be sure. It didn't take long—within an hour, Ginger was thrilled to have a new friend. They were running around, playing, and sharing toys. It was clear they were a perfect match. Once again, Ginger's sweet nature shone through. Similarly, God's mercy can always be trusted—you'll find it holds true time and again when tested.

The ultimate mercy bleed is the person of Jesus Christ. Jesus is the mercy story of Scripture. Interpreting the Scriptures with Jesus Christ in mind puts everything in perspective, giving us a better picture of God. In Jesus,

God's merciful nature is visibly revealed. As Jesus entered the city of Jerusalem before his crucifixion, he wept over it (Luke 19:41-44). Yes, the son of God shed tears over Jerusalem, a city with a reputation for killing its prophets, a city whose residents would kill Jesus. Jesus' lament is recorded in Luke 13:34, *"O Jerusalem, Jerusalem, the city that kills the prophets and stones those sent to her! How often I wanted to gather your children together, just as a hen gathers her brood under her wings, and you would not have it."* The Apostle Paul breaks it down this way, *"While we were yet sinners, Christ died for us"* (Romans 5:8). What we see in Jesus—the tears, the mercy, the love—is what God is. Jesus is the nature of God, shedding tears of mercy for our souls. What an image to have etched in our minds!

From the opening of Genesis' creation poem to the dawn of the New Testament, God's mercy stains the pages of the Bible and each one of our lives. Critics may read this and claim I am over-emphasizing mercy at the expense of God's judgment, suggesting a harsher tone is necessary to motivate people to live moral lives. My go-to defense line is found in James 2:13, where the brother of our Lord says, *"Because judgment without mercy will be shown to anyone who has not been merciful. Mercy triumphs over judgment."* For some time, I have been taken aback by this verse. Particularly the last phrase, *"mercy triumphs over judgment."* According to this verse, the only people subject to judgment are those who receive mercy and decide not to give it. Mercy must not be withheld from another because it is meant to be shared, echoed in Jesus' statement, *"Blessed are the merciful, for they will be shown mercy"* (Matthew 5:7). Sharing mercy instead of hoarding is the most beneficial path for humanity. Those actions reflect the character of

God. Mercy's flow must not be stopped. Mercy received is mercy given in God's economy. It's a river, not a reservoir.

Some believe a stern and judgmental God is necessary to deter misbehavior and prevent moral decay. This perspective argues that without God's harshness, emboldened sinners would cast off all restraint, reminiscent of the days of Noah. Let me point out the flaws in this logic. In my experience, fear of judgment is a poor motivator for behavior change, yielding only short-term compliance. Fear and judgment eventually backfire, as actual change stems from inner transformation, not fear-induced obedience. Genuine character transformation occurs when a person is inspired by a better way of life, reflecting their understanding of God. If God is seen as merciful, loving, and good, people's lives will be shaped accordingly. Conversely, if God is perceived as punitive, guilt-inducing, and frightening, the same shaping occurs, but negatively. I am convinced that positive character traits develop when our understanding of God aligns with goodness and mercy, adorning God's face and following us all our days (Psalm 23: 6).

In a later chapter, I will deal with problematic perceptions that arise from how God's judgment is perceived. But for now, some words of comfort to the hurting seem fitting. To those battered by life's hardships, I extend God's expansive mercy to you. Perhaps your pain's source is from significant people in your life withholding mercy, replacing it with judgment, leading to the recurring theme of personal rejection. Surface-level solutions have been ineffective; deeper care is necessary. Now is the perfect time to receive mercy's healing. The healing salve of God's mercy reaches deep into our souls to places we have yet to unlock. God embodies mercy and heals in ways others cannot. From the beginning of time, God's soul-healing mercy has been a primary source of comfort. It remains humanity's best hope of finding relief. If all you have is God's mercy, you have access to what many generations before you have had, something that continuously flows to the broken places of humanity.

Throughout this chapter, the bleed of mercy has been explored, discovering vivid displays of God's character in the Bible that point people to a healthier way of life. God's reputation is synonymous with mercy, permeating our pain with healing salve. Anchored in attributes of goodness, love, and compassion, God provides a steadfast framework for navigating life's challenges. In the end, mercy triumphs, love conquers, and goodness prevails. Amen!

Spiritual Formation

- What is your concept of mercy? How do you see it running through your life? What story in the Bible illustrates God's mercy for you?

- The phrase *"mercy triumphs over judgment"* from James 2:13 summarizes the New Testament's message in a nutshell. Jesus came to earth as God's merciful servant to triumph over judgment: self-imposed forms of judgment, harmful judgment from the world and its corrupt systems, painful judgments from family and loved ones, and judgments arising from the spiritual enemy of our souls. What specific area of your life needs mercy to overcome judgment? What is your next step to move toward healing and recovery?

- As a recipient of God's mercy, how will you extend mercy to others? What mercy mission might you participate in that relieves others from the evils and injustices that occur in everyday life? Write a specific goal to be a giver of mercy, and find a group of people with whom you can partner to show the face of God's mercy.

- If we are imitators of God, we must show mercy to others. How did you react to the idea of giving mercy as a condition for receiving it? Reflect on Matthew 5:7.

- The bleed of mercy never ceases. It passes through our lives to others, impacting people for generations and leading to wholeness. Are you building a legacy of mercy? How is it taking shape?

Chapter Seven
The face of God who comes near

"The time is fulfilled," He said, "and the kingdom of God is near. Repent and believe in the gospel!" -Mark 1: 15

It's late December at the Hunter compound and my adult children are home for the Holidays. As a family, we will celebrate Christmas Eve at our local church, a tradition we've held for many years. Somewhere in the course of the celebration, the birth of a Savior will be announced. One year, we attended Midnight Mass at a local Catholic parish where the priest shouted, "It's a boy!" to open the service. Christmas is about Jesus, God coming near, and heaven coming to earth. It won't feel that way for people who perceive God as "out there" instead of "down here." For many, God is so different than us, so far away and so mysterious, that a relationship with this God seems far-fetched. Yet, Christmas will be celebrated, and the message of Immanuel, God with us, will enjoy a warm reception whether or not it is something we subjectively experience.

This book strives to address a person's felt concept of God. How we see God is life-shaping. Stated beliefs are important, but the actual operation of faith and how a person sees God in praying, serving, and living are far more consequential. Appropriated faith in the trenches of everyday life is the acid test of any religion. How people feel about God is vital in how they live and treat others. It is incredibly difficult to build a relationship with a distant God. If God is "out there," not "down here" and "with us," then how can this God be genuinely embraced on the level of human intimacy? Following God in vulnerability is an even bigger struggle when God seems a million miles away.

The face of a far-away God is hard to see and even harder to know. The idea that God exclusively resides in a remote location is nothing new. Some belief systems insist God is so far outside of time and space that any knowledge of God is shrouded in a complete mystery. Transcendence is the word used to describe God as a being who exists above and beyond us. This view contrasts the idea of immanence: God with us and among us. In a sense, both are proper indications of who God is. On an experiential level, however, many struggle to grasp God's immanence and nearness because transcendence is the default framework for understanding God. To them, God is up in the sky, detached from earthly affairs. Unless, of course, by praying hard enough and doing good deeds, a desperate plea reaches God, who might respond accordingly. Is God really that way? I'm afraid so, for many. The face of a far-away God is impersonal, demanding, difficult, and not relationally inviting and intimate. It's quite disconcerting when you consider how many people genuinely hunger to know God, but the mystery and ambiguity of a far-away God existing somewhere in the distant sky prevents intimate connection.

This chapter aims to foster fresh perspectives on God's nearness that bridge the divide between heaven and earth. Many people struggle with feeling distant from God. Futile attempts are made to rationalize those feelings away by referencing specific Scripture passages or trying to follow the extravagant claims of preachers and teachers. Rather than deepening one's faith, these approaches often lead to the opposite outcome. Stepping back to acknowledge distant feelings seems like a better path. Something like, *"God, I feel like you are a million miles away and out of touch with my spiritual needs."* King David did just that and recorded it for his readers.

> *How long, LORD? Will you forget me forever?*
> *How long will you hide your face from me?*
> *How long must I wrestle with my thoughts?*
> *and day after day have sorrow in my heart?*
> *How long will my enemy triumph over me?*
> *-Psalm 13: 1-2*

Here, David is struggling with God's hiddenness. Frustrated with God's delays, David feels like God is playing hard-to-get. With unrestrained honesty, the floodgates of his heart open up. *"God, where are you? Please don't make me wait!"* Most of us can relate; when God is most needed, God appears unavailable and out-of-touch, leaving us to feel forgotten and invisible. The inner turmoil and tension are real. David's struggle illustrates the first step in reclaiming a God who is near: boldly confront the perception that God is ignoring us because God is so far away.

Is God really that far away? No, the coming of Christ to earth, called the incarnation, and the abiding presence of the promised Holy Spirit tell us otherwise, but there is more to the story. A person can believe the right things and still feel out of touch with God even though biblical evidence for God's nearness is robust. Operating in that manner of truth, however, is quite another task, and how persons manifest God's nearness is a matter of timing, spiritual readiness, and receptivity. Let me give a poignant example from history.

John Wesley, the great English revivalist, once had a moving encounter with God. As an Oxford-educated Anglican priest, Wesley possessed an impressive pedigree of accomplishments. But all was not well; plagued by doubts, fears, and lack of joy, Wesley struggled mightily with his faith. Until one day, he attended a gathering of Christians at Aldersgate Street in London, at which time God strangely warmed his heart. Like many of us, Wesley's spiritual experience lagged far behind his knowledge base. But in one sacred moment, heaven and earth, experience and reason, transcendence and immanence, collided, producing an epiphany of faith. From there, Wesley preached with new vigor and the message of heart holiness spawned a widespread revival movement. Sanctifying love, complete joy, and nearness to God were characteristics of this movement, and those qualities were seen in the lives of countless thousands of people. While Wesley's struggles were far from over, Aldersgate's watershed moment changed the trajectory of his soul and that of the nation.

The challenge, it seems, is experiencing a God who exists within our time and space and not aloof in the sky somewhere. Wesley's heart-warming experience is one example of many in history. A person's perception of God entering the time and space of human consciousness is stunningly impactful. A single revelatory encounter ushering Wesley into God's presence defined the rest of his life and ministry. For years, he labored for God out of duty instead of delight. He often lamented his soul's pathetic state, crying out to God for deliverance. After Aldersgate, Wesley's relationship with God took on a more intimate tone; he viewed himself as a full-fledged son of the Heavenly Father and not just a servant bound by duty. A heart filled with love and experiential faith made the difference. While God's otherness is a crucial element of faith, we often crave a God who manifests nearness. For Wesley, Aldersgate was that experience. May an Aldersgate experience come to us all!

It's Christmas morning at the Hunter compound. Christmas Day's celebratory essentials are all in place: a decorated tree, stockings on the fireplace mantel, and wrapped gifts for each to open. Not to be forgotten is a prominently placed manger scene in the living room telling the real story of Christmas. Every manger scene offers a different perspective on the events surrounding Christ's arrival. Like seeing God, individuals have the creative license to arrange it as they see fit. The stable may or may not have a covering, the quantity of shepherds varies, and a star is usually found somewhere but not exactly anywhere; everything is subject to interpretation while the Christ Child remains central. The idea that Christ came to dwell among us is the primary message. This is Christmas, Immanuel "God with us," and yes, the presence of Christ among us, assuring our salvation, is of paramount importance—even today.

At Christmas, we celebrate a God who comes to the lowest possible point in order to meet us there and love us (Isaiah 7:14). The Word (Christ) becoming flesh and dwelling among us is how John, the gospel writer, described it (John 1: 14). Jesus, the face of God coming near, is the heart of the Christian faith. God's version of God is embodied in the person of Jesus, who humbles himself, and this is the very essence of what it means to be God (Philippians 2: 1-8). Experiencing that God is the ultimate game changer.

How Jesus came to earth and to whom he first appeared inspire us to draw near to God. The scene at the first Christmas is quite stunning when you think about it. A manger on the outskirts of a small town, an inexperienced mother, dirty shepherds, a panicked father; the list of unusual characteristics and circumstances goes on. Among the first to see the face of God in the form of a child were people of no reputation. God is clearly conspiring with unlikely candidates in Bethlehem. Those the world would consider unqualified stood as instruments of God's choosing. Take note of who was absent at the time of Christ's arrival: the religious elite, socially adept, and politically powerful. As Bethlehem's invitation goes forth, the humble respond. Opposing the proud and giving grace to the humble is how the Christmas story unfolds (Proverbs 3:34, James 4:6, I Peter 5:5). What does this teach? Manifesting the nearness of God begins with a posture of humility. It's the starting point from which we can experience God intimately. Jesus entered the world in humility, not by force, and by so doing, set an example for how we find nearness to God.

We must actively cultivate the ability to experience God's nearness in our lives. You are not alone if you feel distant from God; many do. However, God isn't as far away as you think. Rich pathways and deep practices that fulfill the third phrase of the Triple Prayer, *"to follow God more nearly,"* are available. Deliberate acts of drawing close to God are fixtures in the history of Christian spirituality. Even though God is always present in our lives, heightened awareness and felt nearness are often the result of some form of God-ward movement on our part. The epistle of James eloquently captures this idea, *"Draw near to God, and He will draw near to you"* (James 4:8). Some readers may assume this verse indicates God is not near and summoning God's presence from afar is needed. I don't interpret it that way; it is a statement promoting the idea of awareness. Our responsibility is to adopt spiritual practices that heighten awareness of a God already present in our lives. Let me give an example.

In my work with spiritual formation students, I promote what I call "off-road" disciplines. These practices aim to strengthen our relationship with God outside conventional means and beyond the church's four walls—surpassing routine Bible reading, formal prayers, and corporate worship. Experiencing the rhythms of nature is one such discipline. The crash of waves on a beach, a sunrise over a mountain, a moonlit sky, and the howl of wind on an open prairie are experiences that cultivate greater awareness of God. Nature provides a setting for much-needed prayer, introspection, and growth. Many believers testify to a deeper intimacy with God through encounters with the untamed beauty of creation. I'm particularly fond of off-road disciplines because they ignite my own curiosity and faith formation. Seeing God more clearly, loving God more dearly, and walking with God more nearly are cultivated in life's literal and figurative rough terrain. Spiritual progress often doesn't feel smooth, but the value of going off-road lies in drawing us closer to where God is most active in our lives.

Cultivating nearness to God, regardless of the method, meets very basic human needs because everything about life screams for belonging, intimacy, and attachment. Abraham Maslow famously wrote an essay on the hierarchy of human needs called, *A Theory of Human Motivation*. In it, he created a pyramid diagram to explain how a person's basic needs are prioritized. Intimate relationships and belonging play a big part in human experiences, according to Maslow. The face of a God who comes near fulfills our need for belonging and attachment, making it possible to have healthy relationships with others. Yet, for many persons of faith, God's perceived absence from the human scene leads to feelings of loneliness and isolation. An overly transcendent God who is distant and detached is a difficult God with whom to relate. Those misguided perceptions drive desperate prayers, summoning God to come on the scene and do something heroic. But what if that view of God is incorrect? The true face of God is not just "out there" but "down here." While God's "otherness" is an essential article of faith, God's nearness is vital to love and relationships. Nearness to God is good for the heart and nourishing to the soul. God-with-us reinforces our significance and mitigates our loneliness.

On his deathbed, surrounded by his closest friends, John Wesley repeated these final words: "The best of all is, God is with us." Wesley's Aldersgate experience cemented this idea in his heart, where it remained until his last conscious moment. Declaring God's nearness at the time of his passing couldn't have been more appropriate. A well-lived life is marinated in the idea of heaven coming to earth.

Wesley also reportedly sang the hymn, *"I'll Praise My Maker While I've Breath."* Stunning proclamations from an imperfect man who lived and served as an instrument of God's choosing, much like the characters in the Christmas story. Wesley felt the nearness of God and dedicated his life to seeing the face of God in Jesus.

One final thought: God's presence is life-transforming, extending beyond individuals to entire communities, cultures and nations. The incarnation of God is more than an annual commemoration; it is an unfolding reality in our lives. The early Christians celebrated Christmas over twelve days, and rightly so because it promoted the idea of Jesus' nearness as a continual observance. Each day is an opportunity to cultivate God's presence. It's Christmas all over again!

Spiritual Formation

- For many, God is unknowable and unreachable because God is up in the sky somewhere, unaware of human needs. In other words, there's too much daylight between you and God. What has been your experience with the message of the incarnation? How does the Christmas story address those concerns?

- Cultivating nearness to God begins with taking stock of your spiritual life. For starters, review your daily schedule. Too often, our lives are consumed with distractions and overwhelming responsibilities. As consumed individuals, our souls suffocate and lose perspective on God.

- Are you too busy? How have you carved out time to cultivate nearness? Does your daily routine include designated disciplines that facilitate God-awareness?

- Unresolved emotional turmoil can majorly affect how far away we feel from God because the messiness of human emotions skews our perspective on spiritual matters. How are you doing emotionally? Are you hurt, disappointed, angry? At whom? How did this hurt come about?

- Lastly, examine your personal boundaries. Are you saying yes to people and things when yes is hardly feasible? What about self-care? Do you assume responsibility for others and their happiness while neglecting your needs? At what point are you free to belong to God without taking on the stresses and anxieties of others?

- Write a journal response to these probing questions and develop a plan to address each with specific actions. The goal is to get yourself in the best possible position to see God more clearly, love God more dearly, and follow God more nearly (*Triple Prayer*).

Chapter Eight
The face of a healing God

Do you think God causes pain and human suffering? Some teachers and scholars believe God plays a role, however small, in hurting us in order to heal us. Their view goes something like this: God is in control, and because God is in control, unfolding events in our lives, directly or indirectly, have their origin with God; therefore, God is responsible for bringing them into existence because they ultimately produce good outcomes. When it comes to human pain and suffering, that seemingly innocent belief produces negative views of God. Metaphorically speaking, God is like a vicious pit bull chomping away at our flesh, but God is also the golden retriever compassionately licking our wounds. Interesting visual, isn't it? The images we have of God impact and shape our lives. Let's take it from a different angle: what if we discarded the pit bull image altogether? Suppose God isn't nibbling away at our flesh? Imagine God healing us instead of bringing pain and suffering into our lives. Would that make a difference? I think so.

Some people believe that while God may not be responsible for our pain and suffering, God still uses those things to teach us important life lessons, and there is an element of truth to that claim. They cite passages of Scripture like Romans 8:28, *"And we know that in all things God works for the good of those who love him, who have been called according to his purpose,"* as proof God has a master plan to work everything out for our good, which is admirable and true. Trouble enters the picture when we view God as the being who allows those things to happen, which implies God is the responsible party. Faith journeys turn sour over this assumption because it is scandalous. A God who hurts and also heals is frustratingly difficult for people to reconcile. Considerable tension and inner conflicts arise when both are assumed. Let me give an example.

Sam was raised in a strict Christian home. Ought, should, do, and don't define his faith. In Sam's faith environment, God's sovereignty establishes everything. If one courageously follows God's will, specific blessings accompany a person through life. Pain, displeasure, and even punishment may result if one fails to follow God's will. As Sam became a young adult, he engaged in a relationship with a young lady who did not share his faith tradition's values. After ten years of marriage and the birth of three children, Sam and his wife decided to part ways after several failed reconciliation attempts. Upon finalizing the divorce, Sam suffered from a severe bout of depression. He considered the mental stress as God's way of disciplining him. "If only I had followed God's will, things would be different, and God wouldn't have had to kick my butt," he thought.

Sam's pain-inducing version of God deserves scrutiny. Does God bring pain into our lives, or at the very least, indirectly allow circumstances that lead to depression? Does God ordain harsh consequences for unwise decisions that are somehow part of a bigger plan for our lives? Sam is confused, trying to understand what happened and why. He is not alone; many people struggle with the concept of a God who both hurts and heals. "Everything happens for a reason," they told him, but those words only deepened his pain. The idea that healing is on the way for those who suffer long enough offers no comfort. This perspective suggests God is directly or indirectly responsible for everything because God has a plan that includes events outside God's will. Does God use the ends to justify the means? This viewpoint implies so. Is there a more hopeful path?

Yes, a better path is available if we choose it. Sam's decisions are one thing; his view of God is another. He has two personal battles to fight: healing from a broken marriage and rehabilitating his view of God. Starting with God, Sam might benefit from the first phrase found in the famous Triple Prayer; *"To see God more clearly."* Greater clarity of God's character is a recovery aid. Wisdom to see God as his healer and not as a pain inducer could be the breakthrough for which Sam is looking. The right path is to discern God solely as a source of goodness, love, and mercy. He might also benefit from recognizing other pain sources while assuming personal responsibility for his actions. Let's break down those components, too.

Human pain and suffering are linked to various sources. If God is not the origin of our pain, who or what is? Philosophers and theologians have pondered this question for centuries and found it nearly impossible to find a perfect answer. Identifying the sources of human pain and suffering can be compared to peeling back an onion one layer at a time.

The first layer of the proverbial onion is human responsibility. Adam and Eve's failure in the Garden of Eden illustrates human traits and tendencies to play the blame game. In the wake of the forbidden fruit escapade, Adam shifted blame to Eve and then to God. Blame games hinder spiritual growth and development. God's continued involvement in helping Adam and Eve adjust to the fallen world reveals God's mercy. God was with them in their pain but not the cause of it. The tendency to blame continues today, but something magnificent happens when we recognize our choices belong to us, not anyone else. Take Sam, for example; he was young and in love, not thinking anything could go wrong. Many of us have been there, and despite warnings, we make unwise decisions—even rebellious ones. We cannot heal until we free ourselves from the blame game by taking personal responsibility. Sam's healing journey commenced when he accepted responsibility for his choices. That's one layer.

Acts of intentional harm are the second layer of the onion. Human acts of cruelty toward other humans account for a lot of pain—mean-spiritedness, malice, hostility, violence, etc. Even "religious" people inflict pain on others. The annals of history are full of heartbreaking and regrettable examples. There is no need to expound on meanness other than to say it is a potent layer of the proverbial onion! Sam's marriage started with bliss and romance, but as time wore on, the relationship deteriorated into name-calling with acid words being thrown at each other. Cruel insults came out of his mouth, something he never thought he would do. Wounds were inflicted, and the relationship suffered seemingly irreparable harm.

The presence of evil in the world represents a third layer. A destructive whirlwind of evil forces is at work among us. Like a roaring lion, the spiritual enemy of our soul prowls the earth seeking whom he may devour (1 Peter 5:8). Satan, referred to as the "prince of the air" by the

Apostle Paul, rules this world by commanding evil and influencing people and events (Ephesians 2: 2-4). Yes, God is at war with evil, and this present darkness is so pervasive that it brings a tremendous amount of chaos into our lives. Some faithful Christians use spiritual warfare language to describe the battle between good and evil, which can be very appropriate and Bible-inspired, I might add, so long as it doesn't morph into an obsession with the boogeyman. Living in fear of a devil lurking behind every corner is a burden we can do without. Warring against evil in all its messy and multi-faceted ways is a battle we must responsibly fight. Acknowledging the presence of evil, wherever we find it, is a highly complex layer of the onion that is necessary to peel back. As one might imagine, the spiritual enemy of Sam's soul took great pleasure in the demise of his marriage, seizing the opportunity to lob fiery darts his way.

Human ignorance and weakness add another layer to our understanding of suffering. Despite being the pinnacle of God's creation, humans frequently experience intelligence failures, making terrible mistakes that cause irreparable harm to ourselves and others. The sinking of the Titanic somberly reminds us that even when humanity believes it is at its best, "unsinkable" is not a word we should use. Many tragedies befall innocent people due to human miscalculation, misguided ambition, and misplaced priorities, leading to deadly results. Unintentional harm is a constant companion on life's journey. We've all hit our share of icebergs.

The weakness of our mortal bodies is yet another contributing factor. We are subject to aging, wear and tear, sickness, and disease from the day we are born, and these vulnerabilities put us at a disadvantage. A tired driver veering off the road, an exhausted construction worker falling from a roof, and an overworked physician misdiagnosing an illness all illustrate human frailty. Ignorance of marriage survival skills accelerated the demise of Sam's marriage. Emotional weariness set in from unmet needs and trading insults. Sam's ignorance and human weakness are painfully acknowledged. He is now reckoning with this reality, learning to be an overcomer with greater reliance on a God who heals.

As you can see, the proverbial onion of human pain and suffering has many complex layers. As each layer is peeled, a vivid picture of pain's origin is revealed. Putting a new face on God recognizes the various avenues of pain that are not within God's control domain. By design and because of love, God is not a deterministic being causing all this pain to come into existence. God gives humans the capacity to act freely; sometimes, those activities are met with serious consequences. Since God is loving, merciful, and not controlling and manipulative, a certain amount of liberty in life prevails. That is not to say God sits back with tied hands; God's saving and healing activities go forth with vigor. The face of a healing God comes to us in moments of deep pain, eager to administer the salve of mercy. God's presence in our pain should not be confused with causation. Human weakness, creaturely freedom, the presence of evil, and a fallen world all account for human pain and suffering. To claim God hurts us and also heals is to neglect those considerations. The onion analogy may not explain all pain dilemmas, but most of our suffering can be traced to one layer or another.

Understandably, some will argue that since God created the world and its operation, a certain amount of responsibility is implied. However, I do not make this assumption.

It is more logical to believe in a world where an inherent amount of pain exists apart from God's direct control. God's natural processes, governed by freedom, permit the possibility of painful outcomes, but God does not orchestrate those outcomes. If anything, God actively steers us away from them, not toward them. In this sense, God inspires and influences humans toward good outcomes without forcing us against our will. Influence, not control, is an excellent way to explain God's method.

Does the Bible teach God as a pain source? The biblical record is confident in God's healing but not so confident about God's role in hurting us. Let's examine three samples from the Old Testament to answer the question above. All are drawn from the book of Psalms, where King David reflects on his journey with God. In Psalm 38, David perceives God as a source of punishment and pain.

> *Lord, do not rebuke me in your anger or*
> *discipline me in your wrath.*
> *Your arrows have pierced me, and your hand*
> *has come down on me.*
> *Because of your wrath, there is no health in my body;*
> *there is no soundness in my bones because of my sin.*
> *My guilt has overwhelmed me*
> *like a burden too heavy to bear*
> *- Psalm 38: 1-4*

Piercing arrows, hands descending, and wrath leading to physical weakness—all depicted with vivid imagery. Before jumping to conclusions, it's helpful to identify the literary device at play. David's words, classified as a penitential psalm, eloquently convey human sorrow and remorse over one's actions. In Psalm 38, a context of confession,

God is portrayed as a stern disciplinarian who uses pain as a corrective measure. But does this psalm fully encapsulate God's nature? Is it the definitive statement in David's poetic library? I don't believe so. Fleeting descriptions of God are common in King David's writings. Sorrows, doubts, anger, and emotions pour forth naturally. His words express much personal pain and anguish, but were not meant to be the last word. A snapshot of his spiritual state rather than a permanent conviction is probably a more accurate way of viewing Psalm 38. David is deliberating, not deciding forever that God is one thing or another.

In Psalm 51, King David strikes a different tone. Instead of designating his pain to God, he takes personal responsibility. With mercy as its starting point, David lays bare his soul in brazen honesty. *"Have mercy on me O' God according to your unfailing love, according to your great compassion"* (Psalm 51: 1). Throughout, David focuses on God's mercy while acknowledging his own culpability. In this pivotal moment, he distinguishes between God and the consequences of his own actions without mixing the two at any point. This shift challenges David's prior assumptions, echoing a recurring theme in Scripture—the triumph of goodness and mercy over judgment and wrath. Psalm 51 stands out for this reason, offering a more nuanced portrayal of God. Descriptive language like "unfailing" love and "great" compassion magnify and illuminate God's true character. Psalm 51 doesn't attribute any part of David's pain to God, but God most certainly enters that pain with a gift of mercy.

There are other instances in David's writings where the record is less clear. Take Psalm 103, for example: *"The Lord is full of compassionate and gracious, slow to anger and abounding in love. He will not always accuse, nor will he harbor his anger forever. He does not treat us as our sins deserve, or repay us according to our iniquities"* (vv. 8-10). In this passage, David emphasizes God's compassion and mercy but subtly acknowledges that God's brief anger is still a possibility.

To summarize, King David's descriptions of God range from a God of affliction to a God of complete compassion. We have similar choices when deciding which face we will put on God. Is God a God who afflicts us with pain, or is God a God of prevailing goodness and mercy? If we look at the whole body of King David's work and consider the totality of Scripture, we would have to conclude that a God of mercy and healing prevails despite human perceptions that run wild, accusing God of all kinds of things in which God may not have had any part.

Some readers of the Bible will disagree with me and claim God needs pain and suffering to fulfill a larger-than-life plan for our good. They will cite passages of Scripture like Hebrews 12: 5-6, where the Lord's discipline and chastisement are mentioned. They will insist God has the right to bruise us and break us because those things are spoken in the Bible; therefore, they must be true. They will insist that God's wrath is needed for forgiveness to mean anything at all. At the risk of sounding disrespectful to some faith traditions, I think the face of a God who initiates pain is hazardous to our spiritual health. It seems at odds with how God is experienced in real life and runs counter to a progressing biblical narrative that crescendos with attributes of goodness and mercy and not judgment and wrath. A thickening plot of God's enduring faithfulness and endless mercy grows more evident with the unfolding story of salvation. On that basis, I claim the true face of God is one of total healing, not an unpredictable mix of hurt and healing. This is the God we want Sam to come to know. Sam's version of God didn't hold up to the level of pain he experienced.

For one to experience true healing in this life, the idea of God piercing us with pain is unhelpful. How do we heal from life's wounds while living in fear of the next round of abuse? It's unhelpful because that way of thinking relies on necessary evil, which is problematic on many levels. If the God of our faith reserves the right to kick us in the rear as a harsh method of discipline, how will we ever be free to love this God? It doesn't seem possible for a God of mercy to be the source of our expressed need for mercy. As I see it, a chess match with redemption and healing on one side of the table and hurt and pain on the other doesn't seem like a game God would play. A singular disposition of love seems more likely.

One last thing: does God bring guilt into our lives? My answer may surprise some readers. I think legitimate expressions of guilt flow from a healthy relationship with God. The Bible speaks of the Holy Spirit's conviction and a guilty conscience; neither should be ignored. Have you ever felt unsettled or not at peace about something you've done? Guilt may have been that feeling. While false expressions of guilt can harm our mental state, a guilty conscience can guide moral behavior and heighten our sensitivity to things God cares deeply about. Distinguishing guilt from shame is necessary for good reason. Guilt is the feeling we have because of something we've done or not done. Shame instills the belief we are fundamentally flawed and worthless as human beings. Neither unhealthy guilt nor shame comes from God. However, a nagging sense, "Oops, I've done something wrong," or "I missed something I shouldn't have" is worthy of our attention because it may be God speaking to us. For those reasons, guilt can be good, and God may have a hand in it!

Let me give a personal example. For years, I served as director of a camp program aimed at helping young men grow and develop. A lot can happen in a high-output program where young men try to prove themselves among peers. Every year, a camper or two would shed tears over something. Young men are expected to feel strongly, and opportunities are given to do so healthily. That didn't happen in one instance and one of our campers felt ignored and rejected. When I detected the problem, I immediately felt a sense of failure over what transpired; our values system collapsed and I could not erase that gut feeling in my soul. It was as if God was nudging me to "make it right."

The following day, I apologized to the individual and pledged to do better at living out our community values. It was a freeing experience because the relationship was salvaged, and instead of feeling ignored, the camper in question felt supported. Sometimes, we have to follow our conscience on matters and correct mistakes. I shudder at the thought of how many times I may have missed those opportunities in my life, but you get the idea. An unsettled, even guilty, conscience is not something to dismiss because it can lead to upright human conduct. In that sense, healthy expressions of guilt are positive reminders to be a person of good character. God's way of nudging us to care about the right things is through our conscience. Responding positively to those gut instincts and correcting mistakes further the healing journey for ourselves and others.

Leaving this conversation is difficult because I think of persons like Sam who are experiencing acute levels of pain amid the hard-fought battles they face. For those who perceive God as a source of their suffering, healing from this misconception is crucial. Transitioning from the image of a God who inflicts pain to one whose sole interest is to heal our wounds dissolves a lot of unnecessary confusion, yielding long-term spiritual impact. Exchanging an angry-unpredictable God with one who smiles upon us unleashes new dimensions of joy, happiness, and freedom. Remember that emotional and spiritual healing do not exist in separate domains; they are both deeply tied to how we see God, ourselves, and the world in which we live. Healing from unhealthy images of God is the holy grail of all healing because it raises the bar on what is humanly possible in the realm of wholeness by eliminating burdens that shouldn't be there in the first place.

What is God like? To answer this question we must look beyond conventional thinking and discover the face of a healing God who wants nothing more than our freedom from the enslaving idea that God governs every painful thing that happens to us. If the face of God is punishment, pain, unhealthy guilt, and shame, then we're all going to need intense therapy and hope will quickly turn to despair. Join me in exchanging that version of God for one of mercy and healing. God has come to heal wounds and bind up the brokenhearted, echoed in Jesus' statement, *"It is not the healthy who need a doctor, but the sick,"* (Mark 2:17).

Spiritual Formation

This chapter contains several provocative questions. Don't stress over answering them to perfection. Take some time to reflect on each one. Journal your responses or discuss your perspective in a small group setting.

- Do you think God governs every painful thing that happens to you? What has been your understanding?

- Why do you suppose it is hard for people to grasp the idea that God is not easily angered?

- If God is not the origin of our pain and suffering, who or what is?

- It is difficult to peel back the layers of pain and suffering in our lives. How did the onion-layer analogy impact your understanding of human pain and suffering? Which layer of the onion did you most identify with?

- In what way do you relate to David's writings in the Psalms? Psalm 38:1-4, Psalm 103, Psalm 51

- Does God bring guilt into our lives? How do we distinguish healthy guilt that produces moral character from unhealthy guilt that produces shame?

- In what way does healing from distorted images of God set the stage for healing in all domains of life? How does it raise the bar on what is humanly possible to heal from?

Chapter Nine
The face of justice

> *Yet the LORD longs to be gracious to you; therefore, he will rise up to show you compassion. For the LORD is a God of justice. Blessed are all who wait for him!* -Isaiah 30:18

Are you troubled by the idea of God's justice? Many persons experience some degree of fear and anxiety over God's role as the ultimate justice keeper. Some may imagine God with long white hair, wearing a flowing robe, enthroned on a judgment seat, hearing cases from desperate humans. Anxiety over whether or not this God will show mercy or threaten eternal punishment is the dilemma this creates.

Does God really want us to live in fear of a verdict that might bring dreadful consequences? Or could there be more to the story? Is there a deeper meaning to God's justice? I've taken great pains to suggest that God is genuinely for us, not against us. Because God is always for us, this idea must also apply to justice. As such, justice may be something other than what we fear.

In the preceding chapters, I claim that God's face radiates mercy. Perceptions of God as a stern judge are in stark contrast to this idea. Many contend that sin necessitates a just judge capable of fairly assessing innocence and guilt. They will cite Bible passages depicting God's wrath. This seems to suggest a duality in God's nature: On one hand, God is merciful; on the other, God is a stern judge. Perceptions of God's judgment are mixed, thrilling in one aspect and terrifying in another. God's judgment is thrilling if my enemies are judged harshly. Frightening if God judges me according to the same standard.

The thought of God exercising judgment on human beings is alarmingly complex. How will these judgments pan out? For many Christians, the tensions are hard to reconcile. Does God's face have two sides standing in stark contrast to one another? Is this painful paradox what God intended?

The image of a double-edged sword is a helpful aid in this discussion. A double-edged sword has two sides, like a coin; this is how some people perceive God. Love and mercy are on one side of the sword, and judgment and wrath are on the other. In other words, God's character is two-sided and cuts both ways. God is loving and merciful but also punishing and wrathful. But there's an element of mystery in play. How God shifts from one side of the sword to the other is left to our imaginations. At what point does God get fired up and take a swipe at us using the wrathful side of the sword? Big questions emerge: Is God simultaneously both? Is God really two-faced? For centuries, Christians have had their stomachs in knots trying to explain how God can be one, the other, or both.

This chapter explains why I believe justice and mercy are not two distinct aspects of God but a unified whole. In other words, justice is mercy! I have seldom encountered satisfactory alternatives to the notion of a double-edged sword, prompting a closer look at the subject. Although we may never fully comprehend God's character in this lifetime, we can better understand God's profound attributes and see positive outcomes in our lives.

Many issues and concerns led me to believe the sword has only one edge. First, many believers implicitly embrace double-edged sword thinking, or some form of it, because those beliefs are part of their faith tradition: God is the final arbiter of truth, the cross saves us from God's wrath, heaven is the reward for passing judgment, punishment falls to those living in rebellion, etc. Does any of that sound familiar? Taken to the extreme, some Christians use this version of God as a power play of sorts to obtain status, advance political agendas, and push social values. Prophets of doom, announcing God's judgment if people don't adopt certain beliefs or vote a particular way, are a part of our social experience.

The reputation of Christ and His Church suffer irreparable damage due to these narratives, casting doubt and confusion on unsuspecting believers striving to reconcile a God of mercy with one of justice. Moreover, those inclined toward power will leverage the idea of God's wrath to oppress the vulnerable, as history has shown time and again. Can we live faithfully without projecting God's anger and judgment onto others? I believe so. A God characterized by dualism, with a temper that flares, is not one I can promote, much less worship.

Second, life works so much better from a mental health standpoint when we embrace a God of endless mercy rather than harsh judgment. Like an unhealthy addiction, some believers obsess over the negativity they associate with

God. Have you ever known someone to be critical, spiritually judgmental, or overtly negative about everything? We all have. Sadly, whole movements of Christianity organize themselves around such negativity. When we engage in fearful and aggressive thoughts about God and other people, the human brain responds by producing chemicals that create unhealthy human reactions, frequently resulting in some form of abuse. The clinical aspect is often overlooked, and the unintended health consequences of being a negative person with a negative view of God are observable. While I do not qualify myself as a mental health professional, it is reasonable to assume a fixation on the negative puts the well-being of the mind at risk, possibly leading to patterns of brokenness.

For the sake of illustration and a broader look at how one's view of God as judge affects their living, I'd like to introduce you to Grandpa Fred. Married to his lovely wife Elizabeth for sixty years, Fred raised six children in the church during the post-war era of the 1950s. The church to which he belonged was very conservative. Social activities like movies and dancing were shunned. Sundays were rest days and work was forbidden so the family could attend Sunday School and worship together. Judgmental attitudes and authoritarian beliefs about God were the norm and loyalty to those beliefs was valued. Sex before marriage, divorce, cussing, and alcohol consumption were unacceptable forms of behavior subject to God's strict disapproval. Grandpa Fred's children were raised in this environment, believing God, as a judge, monitored their behavior.

When I served as a pastor, Grandpa Fred, now widowed and ailing, attended my church and was most unpleasant to be around. His children grew to resent his beliefs, and at the time of his passing, little affection remained. Two of his surviving children explained how they wished he were not so controlling and judgmental. Both found healing in a God they discovered was much different than the God of their youth, but vivid memories continued through adulthood. Grandpa Fred inflicted judgment wounds on his children and grandchildren, and with age, his beliefs became more entrenched, more toxic, and more alienating.

For a period of time in our history, Grandpa Fred types filled the pews. Scores of characters like him inflicted judgment wounds stemming from authoritarian judgmental views of God. Grandpa Fred delighted in telling people about the rapture, the second coming, and God's disapproval of unacceptable forms of behavior. He weaponized the Bible and used fear tactics to raise a standard of holiness. Imagine the mental images of God he created in his mind by persistent exposure to such harmful theology. Can this God even be worshipped? If God is a God of punishment, fear, and raw power ruling the universe with an iron fist, Grandpa Fred was in the right and his escalating reign of terror is justified. By now, you have probably figured out from our study that Grandpa Fred's God is not just unhealthy but a fraud.

Figures like Grandpa Fred are hopefully a dying breed with slowing impact, but their influence likely lives on as unspoken values pass down generationally. Misguided understandings of God's justice can be spiritually hazardous, even in subtle forms. The good news is this: if there are people like Grandpa Fred in the world, there are also people who positively embody God's character and contribute to the well-being of others without all the baggage associated with God's judgment. What if God isn't strictly harsh and the metaphorical sword doesn't have two edges?

Why not just one? This is a far more compelling version of God, in my view. God is either all-loving or not God at all, and I can attest to the mental health, emotional wholeness, and positive life outcomes that flow from viewing God this way. I wrote this book to inspire others to view God similarly. Painful paradoxes concerning God's true nature are worth challenging.

I am not the first to speak to these issues, especially regarding a healthy mindset. The Apostle Paul penned the following words to the Philippian church in one of his epistles, *"Finally, brothers and sisters, whatever is true, whatever is noble, whatever is right, whatever is pure, whatever is lovely, whatever is admirable—if anything is excellent or praiseworthy—think about such things"* (Philippians 4:8). In reading this, I am left to wonder, what did the Apostle Paul know about having a healthy mindset that we need to know? Could it be thoughts that determine our lives? Is this wisdom life-changing? I think so, and it most certainly applies to the face we put on God. Our brains think with images, and how we see God has the potential to enhance our thoughts, leading to wholeness. You could say there really is something to "positive thinking." There is no need for negatives to reside where an abundance of positives exists.

A healthy mindset is a byproduct of doing good theology, especially concerning things like God's judgment, which many perceive in an unhealthy manner. Aligning our thinking with God's is a good starting point in any quest to obtain mental health. The word used in the New Testament for judgment is from the Greek word, *krisis,* which implies many different things, the most important of which is a turning point or critical decision resulting in a just outcome. Most would agree that God is the most qualified being in the universe for this action. The relational dimension, however, is often overlooked. Used in its context, *krisis,* as a form of judgment, confirms who is genuinely in a relationship with God. Think of it as a spiritual reveal party where a heavenly spotlight illuminates the relationship choices and condition of humanity while leaving the door open to future faith possibilities. Mercy-filled judgment is an idea I can get behind because it is relationally rich. The Bible speaks of God's judgment, facilitating peoples' turn to God. The *krisis* of God is not just revealing; in the sense that it discloses destinies already chosen, it is revealing because it keeps the door open invitationally. The relational component is strong but often ignored in favor of punitive meanings, which close the door.

Only a qualified judge can reveal something as complicated as the world's spiritual condition. Jesus is God's instrument for this activity, and He gave us clues about how that activity is handled. *"Many will say to me on that day, 'Lord, Lord, did we not prophesy in your name and in your name drive out demons and in your name perform many miracles? Then I will tell them plainly, 'I never knew you. Away from me, you evildoers!'"* (Matthew 7:23). A relational tone is struck with these remarks. Spiritual reveal moments sort out phonies and hypocrites. People routinely claim to represent God but clearly do not. They will insist they are doing God's work and purport to have God's Spirit when nothing could be further from the truth. We might call this exposure judgment. The reveal moment unveils the truth about which individuals genuinely follow God and which are faking it. In that sense, we can find rest in the justice of Christ, which always seems to identify people we least expect to be in God's kingdom. Surprising outcomes are tied to God's judgment, particularly the vindication of the innocent and the elevation of the most vulnerable.

God's judgment is really a scandal of goodwill when you think about it. May God give us many impactful reveal moments!

I'm sure some reading my thoughts will have doubts; they might insist I am merely putting a positive spin on God's judgment to prove my thesis of a kinder and gentler God. They may claim God does have a bent toward anger, and a vengeful God is needed to deal with brutal dictators and evil-doers whom we all agree need to be held accountable. The scenario of ultimate justice has a lot more to do with the natural consequences of removing oneself from God, which is pretty tragic in itself, as opposed to fury and wrath coming down from heaven. In the parables Jesus spoke, where rich images describing the administration of justice are found, evil-doers, hypocrites, and other bad actors are not regarded as belonging to God or worthy of standing in God's presence (Matthew 25, Luke 12: 8-9, Luke 13: 22-25). The painful reality of being out of God's presence by choice is met with harsh outcomes, and if those self-inflicted wounds aren't punishment enough, I don't know what it is. The God of the New Testament doesn't seem hellbent on anyone's destruction. Pending executions, divine punishment sprees, and harsh judgments do not appear to be in line with what God seeks to accomplish in the administration of *krisis*.

The beauty of *krisis* is its respect for human will, which reflects God's nature of love. God grants humans autonomy; they make their own choices, and unfortunately, many of those decisions lead to despairing results. Divine reveal moments aren't opportunities for God to have an angry flare-up and dispense punishment. Instead, they serve as moments of profound awakening orchestrated by a merciful judge whose wisdom surpasses our own and whose judgments are inherently fair. I don't know about you, but I'm good with that because everything God does is an expression of mercy that honors people's will while spurring them toward greatness. Spiritual reveal moments are actually designed to help me see what I need to change and why. They exist to bring down barriers in my relationship with God and produce transformation. The purpose is redemptive!

Even within popular culture, the significance of game-changing reveal moments is recognized. Affectionately dubbed "Come to Jesus" moments, these instances mark the sudden realization of a glaring truth. Can you think of a time when you realized you were not joined with God and something needed to be done? Other types of life experiences may also fit into this category. If we are suddenly awakened to something previously hidden and it alters our life path for the better, God is part of that glorious work. Sudden moments of revelation are for our good because God is good. Reveal moments, if we respond positively, force us out of the limitations we placed on ourselves and fuel vibrant personal growth. Different labels exist for this phenomenon: aha-moment, gestalt, personal epiphany, wake-up call, watershed moment, and more. Regardless of terminology, the journey from who we are to who we're becoming is adorned with such moments.

To put the final wrap on our double-edged sword analogy, I'm not a double-edger because I believe the New Testament teaches differently. If there are two equal sides to God's character standing in such stark contrast, we may need to re-read the text and re-examine Jesus. The whole characterization of it is flawed. It portrays a dual-natured God. I cannot uphold the double-edged sword theory for those reasons and others. While we cannot take one verse from the Bible and explain everything, I have taken great liberty to call your attention to James 2: 13 where a poignant reminder is found; *"Mercy triumphs over judgment."*

This little nugget of wisdom tucked away in the short epistle of James is yet another signpost that points to God's most basic intention. Mercy lies at the heart of everything God does. And think of it: God's mercy will outlast ill-fated human judgments from which so many of us have suffered. Rest assured, someday God, the final judge, will exercise merciful *krisis* and the dark psychology of God's punishing nature will be banished forever. As time unfolds, moments of revelation will happen, and hidden things will be unveiled, moving us toward a deeper connection with God. Whatever judgments you perceive as coming from God, consider they may not be as harsh as you think because the face of justice and the face of mercy are one and the same. A relational God exuding love exercises judgment, and it is benevolent.

I do not stand alone in claiming God's justice is relational kindness. Frederick William Faber (1862), an English cleric, composed a hymn entitled *"There's a Wideness in God's Mercy,"* highlighting the idea lyrically. In verse one, he writes, *"There is a wideness in God's mercy, like the wideness of the sea, there is a kindness in his justice, which is more than liberty."* Faber also touches on false human perceptions of God, *"We make God's love too narrow by false limits of our own, and we magnify its strictness with zeal God will not own,"* (verse 3). Such powerful statements! God always has a voice coming through every generation, speaking to the vastness of God's love and the nature of God's kindness. Verse 4 of Faber's hymn elaborates further, *"For the love of God is broader than the measures of the mind, and the heart of the Eternal is most wonderfully kind."* The power of kindness, the potency of love, the greatness of mercy—ideas that, when put into practice, truly convert humanity. Strictness, punishment, and pending execution are not motivators for any healthy relationship, let alone a relationship with God.

One crucial aspect to consider is how putting the right face on justice translates into higher levels of human responsibility. Instead of placing the burden of the world's injustices solely on God, we are called to share in the responsibility. In Matthew 25, Jesus' most significant parable on judgment, a call for action goes forth to help those in need. This reflects God's vision of justice—working through the faithful, not by imposing force. Those who cling to a dark view of God's judgment often dismiss human involvement, believing that "God will eventually fix everything." However, embracing the true image of God calls for faithful action, not passivity. It means taking seriously our stewardship and the pursuit of justice in the world. We might ask ourselves: If God is working to reveal these opportunities, what is our response? How are we promoting reconciliation and healing? This shift moves us from a stance of passivity to a position of self-accountability, and divine calling. As imitators of God, we must engage in the work of justice, just as God does.

Spiritual Formation

- Describe a time of feeling judged by another person. How did you react? How did you resolve the judgment wound? Or, what can you do now to heal?

- How does the face of justice give you hope? Identify some outcomes from a God of mercy and justice at the helm of the universe.

- Take an inventory of your thought life. What negative things do you let yourself dwell on? How can you turn your thoughts, especially your thoughts about God, in a more positive direction?

- God's mercy reflects God's love and does all the incredible things we long for. It heals, restores, conveys hope, etc. Where is God's mercy most needed in your life?

- The invitation to come and see the face of God glimmering with mercy and exuding love is yours. To explore this concept further, the following scriptures are suggested. Psalm 23, Psalm 103, Micah 6: 6-8, Matthew 5:7, Hebrew 4:16, Isaiah 30: 18

- How might the power of kindness, the potency of love, and the greatness of mercy transform the spiritual health of your relationships, including your marriage and faith community?

- As imitators of God, we, too, must seek justice. How is justice carried out responsibly? Whom does it benefit the most? Describe what faithful action looks like in your setting.

Chapter Ten
Helping others put a new face on God

If one thing is true about God, it is this: God is not discouraged by humans struggling to see God more clearly. God actively reaches into the blurry-faced messes we've created with a steady flow of grace-giving clarity. Despite the dimly lit graves we dig for ourselves, God still reveals, speaks, and moves on our behalf. When we reciprocate that movement in the spirit of the famous Triple Prayer, we will have more vision, intimacy, and purpose in our relationship with God. This book has focused heavily on the "seeing" aspect of faith because the face we put on God is crucial in spiritual formation. God wants to be seen and welcomes our gaze. Fixing our eyes on Jesus, the perfect representation of God, is the faithful's call. God is not upset when we falter in this pursuit; instead, God is relentless in granting measureless revelation. As one biblical writer said, *"God is the rewarder of those who diligently seek him"* (Hebrews 11:6).

As our view of God improves, so does our peace of mind and level of humanity. This transformation is not just for personal benefit; it is a mission to help others. Your engagement in the mission can be infectious and life-changing to the people around you. Too often, blurry face versions of God prevail, leaving people in a state of spiritual ruin. The carnage is felt at all levels of society. Reversing the damage is no easy task, yet profound hope lies in a God who is faithful through the ages and whose grace knows no bounds. Guiding others to experience the heights and depths of endless mercy is a sacred calling. Where do we start?

The listening side of love is a fitting place. Permitting people to share their view of God without fear of a counterargument is a crucial step. The open-ended dialogue approach yields better results than correcting, critiquing, and debating. People genuinely need a sanctuary to wrestle with their views while considering other possible perspectives on God. When you establish an atmosphere of trust and a willingness to listen lovingly, the quality of what is shared rises significantly. Ask yourself: *Am I someone who can be trusted? Am I patient enough to listen without interrupting? Will people wrestling to overcome negative views of God feel I am someone with whom they can divulge their spiritual doubts and frustrations?*

Becoming a great "listening" friend is a strategy that never goes out of style. Create conversations that make your struggling friends the most important persons in the room, not you, the listener. Alert yourself to the fact their stories may include some pretty heavy stuff. Be prepared to hear gut-wrenching, heartbreaking stories illustrating the hurt, pain, and disappointment associated with harmful views of God. Spiritual abuse is rampant within the Christian Church and society in general. Exposure to people who abuse, manipulate, and leverage God-talk for their own personal agendas is very high. Feeling angry and upset at people of religious faith who permitted the continuation of trauma and abuse is completely understandable. I've felt that way many times myself. However, your calling and mine, is to facilitate a healing presence and display a way of living and being that exudes the goodness of God. Others need our kindness and grace, showing them the possibility of God's grace despite the confusion they have encountered. Becoming a "listening" friend and not leaving the relationship demonstrates love in action, which is a true reflection of God's face.

For many years, I served as an online professor, preparing students for various types of Christian service; most students were female. Many hailed from very conservative churches in the Midwest and South, where women were ineligible for ordination based on their gender. It begs the question: What kind of God would do this? A bigoted and sexist God? Some recounted excruciating stories of pain and rejection from this harmful practice. Others did not question male headship and submitted to the long-held tradition of putting men in charge of everything. Private online forums were safe places for students to wrestle with their call while discerning God's character. Engaging in conversations with a broader opinion base and wider interpretation of the Scriptures proved helpful. For many women, resistance came from their own gender and even members of their own family. I am still taken aback by the number of people who claim to follow the Jesus of the Bible and discount the role of women, something Jesus never did. An online forum with like-minded individuals allowed students to make refreshing new discoveries while considering a new narrative and possibly a different view of God.

While the gentle approach usually persuades when it comes to helping people put a new face on God, a good old-fashioned "nudge" is also appropriate. Unlike giving unsolicited advice, nudging is less intrusive. It is more consistent with a prompt, a suggestion, or a thoughtful presentation of an alternative view. It is not a demand or an ultimatum. People's view of God is a delicate matter and the faces they put on God are tied to experiences and understandings that are deeply personal. It is better to nudge than risk pushing people away to the point of retreat. When people are pushed and propelled with any degree of force, they respond in ways that are emotionally reactive instead of rational. They say and do things they would not normally do. They react to you instead of responding to the unveiling work of God. Nudging is a loving action sown into the fertile ground of a receptive heart. Nudging enlightens, enriches, and encourages the adoption of seeing God in a better light. Nudging people along their journey with open-ended questions, gentle prods, positive suggestions, and constructive solutions is desperately needed. "Nudge, but don't fudge" is timely advice for all. We can challenge harmful assumptions about God without ruining relationships; gentleness doesn't mean silence. It actually allows one to speak with profound impact and volume.

What do we do when people double down on their view of God? Very candidly, we step back. No task is more defeating than trying to fix people's beliefs or control their thoughts; this is not the way of love. Sometimes we have to sit in discomfort among people with whom we have a relationship, acknowledging that they are not where we want them to be. For reasons I cannot fully understand, some people double down on harmful views of God despite all the evidence to the contrary. They may have fears of betraying a God they have come to understand, and whether or not that God is even real is irrelevant. It is real to them because a person's perception is a hard-core reality. Perceptions of God are created with great ease, and holding onto those perceptions can also be a matter of personal pride. There may be social and religious reasons for sticking to a particular version of God. Discomfort with the deeply held views of others does not necessarily mean exiting the relationship, though severing ties may be required in some instances of abuse. Instituting appropriate personal boundaries and attitudes of tolerance can save the day in most settings. When doubling down happens, don't be discouraged; it may be a cue to double down in grace.

How do we deal with someone who possesses an unhealthy version of God and belongs to a religious cult? Cult is such a harsh word; I prefer "high control." Many religious groups threaten members with excommunication should they no longer live in accordance with certain doctrines of God. I wish it were not true, but dogmatic reigns of terror abound. One of the diagnostic features of high-control religious groups is the intolerance of outside beliefs. Members are instructed to be suspicious of other beliefs about God. Sadly, the authoritarian, intolerant face they put on God fosters division and separation, and nothing could be more relationally harmful. People stuck in those belief systems fear the religious authorities, predominately men, under whom they serve. If you have a relationship with someone in a high-control religious tradition, take great pains to understand their need for friends outside of that social grouping. They may need you someday!

A genuine friend prioritizes the relationship over deeply ingrained religious differences, choosing unity over division. Even amidst disdain for differing perspectives on God, it's essential not to neglect the opportunity for dialogue. Perhaps in the future, when rigid beliefs soften and dogmatic convictions crumble, there may be room for a richer and more vibrant journey together, yielding unity and love. Until then, remain available to those individuals.

Healing communities are another vital component in helping people put a new face on God. Communities, not just individuals, heal people. You as an individual may effectively advocate for someone to develop healthier spiritual practices that help them put a new face on God, but if that person fails to experience healthy Christian community, they will likely wander in directions that lead away from faith and maturity. As a life principle, people are best helped in relationships with others. This is God's way of forming us into a better version of ourselves. Christian communities who understand the value of individual choice are best suited for healing activity. Coercion of any kind, forcing one's view on another, contradicts the ways of love and fails to advance healing activity. People are hungry for authentic communities of faith where respect, kindness, and freedom-giving love are guiding principles. The primary function of a faith community is to heal, not forcibly indoctrinate.

As a healing community, make specific appeals to people who are struggling. At my home church in Arizona, we have set out to do just that. Our mission is clear: *"The people of Crossroads exist to show absolutely everyone that God is good."* We hope this communicates our best intentions for people as they become a part of our worshipping and serving community. God's kindness, tolerance, and faithfulness are at the core of our messaging. As we become better storytellers of God's goodness, a spirit of contagious optimism spreads to those looking to trade a burdensome view of God for one that is uplifting and transformative.

Some final thoughts. Reflecting the image of God is a universal calling. You may not have formal training or authority to present God to others, but you can do the Lord's work in helping people put a new face on God. It begins with the story of redemption unfolding in your heart. Your life becomes a tangible mirror reflecting who you know God to be. Your perception of God forms your outlook and perspective on life, which is infectious and influential on those within your reach. When this authenticity shines through, a silent sermon unfolds without saying a word. Having read this book and engaged in this conversation, you can now be a storyteller of God's goodness, partnering with God to bring about a new version of humanity!

Spiritual Formation

- How would you rate your ability to listen to people on a scale of 1-10, with 10 being the most outstanding listener? How would other people rate you? Ask someone you trust and compare the differences.

- Assess your relationships with people who may have different perspectives on God; how do you find common ground? What can you celebrate together? How do you manage those differences without leaving the relationship?

- High-control religious groups often devalue individual choice. What does that reveal about their view of God? How would you advise someone belonging to such a group? Remember Grandpa Fred from an earlier chapter? What are your thoughts about the church to which he belonged?

- Healing communities value listening and individual choice. What does this look like in the context of relationships? How do we live out faithfulness to the church's mission without smothering people and pressuring them to accept certain propositions?

- To be an intentional healing community, one must set specific goals. Work on a mission statement like the one presented in the chapter by Crossroads Church. What can you set out to achieve that will help people recover from religious communities that hurt instead of heal?

- What kind of person is a storyteller of God's goodness? What sets them apart? How are they different from some religiously schooled people?

- People tend to reflect who they understand God to be. As our view of God improves, so do our lives because imitating the goodness attributes of God leads to wholeness. Channel this idea into a personal prayer and record it as a journal entry. Putting a new face on God and becoming an imitator of God's likeness must be marinated in prayer.

Chapter Eleven
Final blessing: The face of God shines now and forever

Sharing a benediction is the most fitting way to end our conversation, and it does my heart good to leave you with one with such rich meaning. The "shining face" reference is drawn from an Old Testament passage of Scripture in the book of Numbers called the Aaronic blessing. It is a proclamation declaring something about God that will impact people's lives. The Lord directed Moses to tell Aaron and his sons—who were the priests—to bless the Israelites and say to them:

> *The LORD bless you and keep you; the LORD make his face shine on you and be gracious to you; the LORD turn his face toward you and give you peace*
> *-Numbers 6: 22-26*

Moses delivered this message from the Lord to Aaron and his sons as a priestly blessing; these words have echoed throughout Jewish history to the present day. Appreciating the English equivalent of Hebrew words translated bless, keep, shine, gracious, and peace is somewhat challenging to the modern mind. Be assured that in their original context they carried a lot of weight. The real beauty is seen in what these words reveal about God's character. In Hebrew, a face represents the totality of a person's being, just like the face of any human being. Imagine God's shining face looking upon you with favor. All that God is in glory, splendor, and wonder noticing a person like you. What an incredible thought! The totality of who God is, beaming with hope and exuding love, shining like a star over every aspect of our existence. Stunning to think about!

God's shining face is a message that needs urgent hearing. The erosion of the Christian Church in the Western hemisphere has significantly disrupted the faith of many devoted believers. The very organism charged with the task of delivering the message of good news has stumbled. Older generations of Christians are faltering and younger generations are abandoning the faith. What's happened? A comprehensive answer to that question goes way beyond the scope of this book, but one issue I would like to address. The dark and scary images the Christian Church has traditionally used to portray God have backfired. Instead of a God too beautiful and compelling to resist, we have settled for bloody images of a Christ who bore punishment on a cross to appease God. Striking Jesus down in cold blood to satisfy God's wrath is that message. Images of a stern, angry, and unpredictable God have had a chilling effect on Christian spirituality, emptying our churches and gutting our souls. Thankfully, a new version of God is being born, even as I write. A God whose face shines so bright the dark images of judgment and wrath pale in comparison.

The shining face of God has many practical applications. One, in particular, is how it may help us deal with the problem of human shame. In all its various forms, shame is that awful feeling of inadequacy, humiliation, and embarrassment. Some experts define shame as a psychological and spiritual response to the absence of love because shame reinforces the idea that something is inherently wrong with me that makes me unlovable. Shame sufferers often feel they have nowhere to turn and there is a scarcity of resources available to find relief. Not everyone can be treated by a professional. The magnitude of people's suffering demands a spiritual solution that exceeds the limitations of modern therapy. I believe a new version of God can effectively treat shame. The next time you feel awful about yourself and loathe your identity as a human, look in the direction of God's shining face and find people who can support you in fixing your eyes on a vision of God that heals from shame's deepest wounds.

God's shining face is a potent force in canceling human shame. Let me explain how. When we look upon the face of mercy and embrace a God of love, a framework for dealing with shame is firmly set. Too often, the framework we adopt to address human shame does not hold up, and sufferers circle the wagons, running from treatment to treatment, therapist to therapist, church to church, relationship to relationship, in search of something to adequately address how they feel about themselves. A framework of healing built on a foundation of love flowing from a God whose good nature is the very source of life makes shame recovery possible. Don't we all want to see God's shining face as we deal with shame's dehumanizing effect on our souls? I can't think of anything more stabilizing to our inner lives.

There's another level of application worth mentioning. The deep wounds of shame often come from the institutions and organizations to which we belong. Shaming an individual or a group can be profoundly painful, whether from a church, a corporate organization, or a family system. These wounds run deep because our identities and livelihoods are tied to these relationships. Institutions often lack empathy, and to survive, they may resort to shaming tactics, cannibalizing their own members. This leads to self-devaluation which can take years to overcome. Have you ever been fired? Denied a promotion? Pushed out of a church? Or experienced blatant rejection from a peer group? Many of us have. Institutions and systems don't love you the way God loves you, even when they claim to represent God.

A vertical shift in life focus can minimize the trauma of these shaming wounds. Finding the courage to lift our eyes to God's shining face despite the abuse, rejection, and shame inflicted upon us by the institutions to which we belong is imperative. Imagine loving a God who cancels our shame through unconditional love, acceptance, and forgiveness. So unlike the systems of this world. Victims of abuse, shame sufferers, and people struggling to find their identity desperately need this hope. Deeply embedded shame wounds are among the most difficult from which to heal. An enormous amount of professional counseling, healing resources, and attention are aimed at addressing this human need. Where those resources leave off, God's shame-canceling love is available.

God's shining face is also essential as we navigate through unusually difficult seasons in our lives. Several years ago, we lost both my father and my father-in-law within a short span of time, plunging us into a challenging period of loss. The mental illnesses from which they both suffered further complicated matters, burdening us with travel, care management, and legal issues in resolving their estates. Looking back, I often think, "Wow, I went through all that?" I can't imagine enduring difficult seasons while believing they were divinely orchestrated to make me a better person. That notion feels cruel and incompatible with a God of love. Instead, the shining face of God reassures me, especially in my darkest hour, that the source of all things good has my best interests at heart.

The comfort I draw comes from Hebrews 4:16, where believers are invited to approach God confidently in our time of need. Far too many have shaken confidence in approaching God due to the debilitating perceptions they carry, but God's invitation remains. The invitation to approach God confidently comes to us in times of sadness, grief, and lament. It comes to us in moments of brokenness when we have nowhere else to turn. It comes to us when our perceptions of God leave us dissatisfied and searching for more. The invitation is to go directly before God and obtain mercy, knowing that the source of all things good is found there. The audacious hope of this book is that you will be awakened to God's shining face, no matter where you find yourself on life's journey and despite what you are experiencing.

Following Jesus' resurrection from the dead, there was a forty-day interlude before His ascension to heaven. Jesus appeared to many in the resurrected bodily form, including His closest followers. If I lived at the time Jesus lived, I would have wanted to encounter him this way. It fascinates me to no end that Jesus was the face of God, standing in our midst, beckoning us to behold His resurrected glory. At any rate, Jesus went with His followers to the

Mount of Olives before ascending into heaven. The Bible tells us that he lifted both hands and proclaimed a blessing over them. What was that blessing? Some Jewish scholars believe the blessing he pronounced, though not explicitly noted in the text, was none other than the Aaronic blessing. How fitting! We know the response was immediately positive. According to one gospel writer, *"They worshipped Him, and returned to Jerusalem with great joy, and were continually in the temple praising and blessing God"* (Luke 24:52). May God's shining face be yours to behold now and forever. Amen.

Spiritual Formation

- Write out the blessing from Numbers 6:24-26. Spend at least five minutes reflecting on the words.

- Substitute your name for each pronoun that refers to a person as you read the Scripture out loud.

- How does your perspective of God and yourself change as you personalize the blessing?

- Ponder the potential of blessing others with the shining face of God. What does that look like? Does that include people you may have overlooked? What about your enemies?

- What could God's shame-canceling love mean for you? Where is it most needed in your life?

Chapter Twelve
Today's big question: What is God like?

I hope you found answers to this crucial question while reading this book. Understanding God more clearly is a lifelong journey, often easier said than done. High levels of spiritual abuse and misguided interpretations of God have left many in need of healing conversations. For someone raised in an abusive home with an authoritarian father who weaponized the Bible, the journey must start somewhere. Shifting from associating God with abuse to seeing God as a loving presence is a challenging process that can take years. However, the journey is worthwhile, as our perception of God shapes our lives. Positive transformation occurs when we truly understand who God is and let go of unhealthy views that compound our problems and impede our journey toward Christ-likeness.

Wherever you find yourself on the path to a better understanding of the nature and character of God, I pray the words and stories in our study will hearten you. I could not have written this book earlier in my life because I would not have had the vantage point of wrestling with these issues over three decades. I'm still reflecting on God, a process that will continue until I take my last breath. The face I put on God is far more loving, patient, and understanding than the face of God in my youth. As a young man with a Type "A" personality, I was uncertain of God's identity. A part of me wanted to embrace a God with the ferocity of a warrior and the control of a dictator. At times, angry-authoritarian versions of God flooded my mind that needed to be overcome. Impoverished views of God are common in the early stages of faith formation. We gain perspective with time and human suffering.

What changed my views? Marriage, the birth of children, writing a dissertation, the death of loved ones, the decline of the Church, wounded people, ministry failures, chronic health issues, etc. Sometimes better views of God are born in hardship. All of life has formative value, and everything that happens shapes us for good or ill. I saw God more clearly in my suffering, which helped me more readily exchange images of God as a warrior for a God of love and empathy.

In this book, I have delicately criticized traditional venues of Christianity for their failure to bear witness to the true image of God. Please understand that I love the Church, and the local church to which I belong has my devotion and support. My support, however, does not in any way condone the harmful images of God projected on others by the Church. In light of these difficulties, I strive to partner with like-minded people to bring about change. Correcting impoverished views of God involves offering new insights deeply rooted in our past with present-day relevance. Too often, the version of God presented in the conventional setting of the Church is male-only, violent, overtly political, and transactional: A God too small and unloving to worship. New and refreshing views of God are being born everywhere in the hearts of men and women inside and outside the Church. I am not the first to embark on this mission and certainly won't be the last. As with much of Christian history, there is ebb and flow, death and rebirth, and darkness and light. Rediscovering God's true image is a new awakening that promises to fortify our faith, revive our churches, and enhance our mental health.

I know this to be an authentic movement because God is not without a witness. Like cream rising to the surface in a container of raw milk, the best and most worthy versions of God naturally rise to the top. Despite Christianity's pitfalls, and there are many of them, God's version of Godself will always rise, capturing hearts and changing lives. The writer of Acts speaks to this reality, *"Yet he has not left himself without testimony: He has shown kindness by giving you rain from heaven and crops in their seasons; he provides you with plenty of food and fills your hearts with joy"* (Acts 14: 17). There is no escaping God's goodness. It is always present and noticeable despite the blurry-faced images of God that are so prevalent in our minds.

God's true face shines through no matter how dark or despairing our moments may be. Characteristics of goodness, mercy, and self-giving love are the cream rising to the top. God's revelation and self-disclosure will break forth in the hearts of receptive people. At no time in history has God remained hidden, and at no time in our future will God be without a spokesperson. Saints testifying to the goodness attributes of God have reliably spoken through the ages and will continue to speak. Their voices rise when whole populations of people are restricted from free worship. They cry out when innocent children die of starvation while the rich exploit the earth for lavish living. They fervently speak when so-called leaders who claim to represent God oppress entire nations. The true face of God is seen in the hearts of those who know God and want to make God known in word and deed. Even if they are few in number, they delight in seeing light overcome darkness and goodness conquer evil. They relish opportunities to spread the good news that God is for us, and though there may be many messages to the contrary, resolve to proclaim the good news of God's glimmering face remains steadfast.

Some may have read this book and still struggle to answer the big question of what God is like. Don't give up! Much of what I have shared has grown from my experience of engaging hundreds of students over the last decade, and if I learned anything from my teaching role, it is that everyone sees God differently. The face we put on God is unique to each of us. I may not have been able to communicate with everyone sufficiently, but I am happy to spur you onto greener grass in hopes you find a worthy version of God wherever it can be found. Bear in mind the journey of discovery is long and requires diligence and humility—eventually, you will get there. God is no respecter of persons, and the invitation remains to come boldly to the throne of grace, *"Let us then approach God's throne of grace with confidence, so that we may receive mercy and find grace to help us in our time of need"* (Hebrews 4: 16). God is not hiding from us. Instead, God is eager to disclose everything we need to enjoy a rich life of love and service to others.

The end is really the beginning. I submit an imperfect book with an incomplete account of my thoughts and reflections on God. These pages contain the record of one person's journey; my words are a snapshot of a bigger picture unfolding. The conversation continues. From here, the face we put on God can only get better. There is no such thing as an unfiltered, uninterpreted account of God. We have to work at it, and we have everything to gain. The Apostle Paul encourages us on our journey with these timeless words, *"I keep asking that the God of our Lord Jesus Christ, the glorious Father, may give you the Spirit of wisdom and revelation, so that you may know him better"* (Ephesians 1:17). Paul prays the Ephesian Church will get to know God better. Knowing God better includes seeing God in better light with the spirit of wisdom and revelation. That's my prayer for you as you read this book's last page. Blurry-faced versions of God abound, but the lucidity of hope is alive, and the work of changing our inner perceptions of God goes forward. As our vision of God increases, so does our quality of life and ability to serve others.

If this book has positively impacted your view of God, I am beyond grateful. Any progress in your spiritual journey, I attribute to God. I also have a humble request: your recommendation would mean the world to me. I wrote this book for my children on a tight budget, unsure of who might be touched by its unique message. Success depends on readers like you sharing it with others. Will you help spread the word about *"Putting a New Face on God"?* I sincerely hope, my goal is to aid as many people as possible in seeing God more clearly. Remember the wisdom shared by a Catholic priest in the first chapter: "It's not preposterous to believe in God—it's preposterous to believe in a preposterous God."

Afterword

If you know anything about Bob Hunter, you likely know that his ventures that often involve adrenaline rush, outdoor sports, do-it-yourself projects, his dog Ginger—and creative, funny and often zany YouTube videos. But integrated into every facet of his life is his passion for Jesus and his love of a relational God.

I first got to know Bob, a seminary trained pastor, about 20 years ago when we ended up on a volunteer team together that created weekly study guides for small groups at our church in Gresham, Oregon. Our goal was to write questions that would encourage people to wrestle with Scripture and figure out how it applies to relationships with God and others. Bob and I often had long conversations about practical ways to help others learn about Jesus and what helpful discipleship methods might look like.

After Bob moved to Arizona with his family, he took action on his dream to disciple young men through a not-for-profit he called Rip'd4Life. We still keep in touch and he often asks me to critique and edit articles and other discipleship tools he develops as he mentors young men in practical life skills partnered with what a life looks like lived for Jesus. I appreciate that Bob wrestles with his own faith as he mentors and engages with others; he also asks provoking questions that challenge me to think differently about living in relationship with Jesus.

Afterword

As an experienced facilitator of Bible-focused small groups and healing/recovery small groups, I have learned a lot about the residue behaviors and patterns left in our brains—including my own—from trauma, misinformed or unhealthy parenting, relationships that have left us with low self-worth, cultural influences, intended or unintended mis-use of Scripture, and our own interpretations of our experiences. Without awareness and intentional pursuit of change, all those influences can hinder ability to grow toward mental, emotional and spiritual health.

Bob's book addresses what gets in the way of developing an emotionally and spiritually healthy relationship with God, and is based on what I believe is accurate biblical theology. When Bob proposed writing a book about the blurred images our brains may have created as we "see" God, I was eager to have a new vocabulary and narrative to help myself and others think through our own perspectives of God. Discarding false images of God that are imbedded in our brains and replacing those with a biblically accurate Face of God will lead to a more intimate relationship with God. That new Face of God unblurred will allow us to not only know about God but to also believe the God who is deeply in love with us.

Linda Dodge

MA in Pastoral Ministry (Multnomah Biblical Seminary); a passionate focus on learning about Jesus and relationships in the Gospels; specialties include group facilitation & communication skills

Made in the USA
Monee, IL
22 February 2025